ROAST FIGS
SUGAR SNOW

"*In the morning the house was warm from the stove, but when Laura looked out of the window she saw that the ground was covered with soft, thick snow. All along the branches of the trees the snow was piled like feathers, and it lay in mounds along the top of the rail fence, and stood up in great, white balls on top of the gate posts. Pa came in, shaking the soft snow from his shoulders and stamping it from his boots. 'It's a sugar snow,' he said.*"

LITTLE HOUSE IN THE BIG WOODS   LAURA INGALLS WILDER

ROAST

FIGS

SUGAR

SNOW

WINTER FOOD TO
WARM THE SOUL

DIANA HENRY

PHOTOGRAPHS BY JASON LOWE

Roast Figs, Sugar Snow by Diana Henry

First published in Great Britain in 2005 by
Mitchell Beazley, an imprint of
Octopus Publishing Group Limited,
2–4 Heron Quays, London E14 4JP.

Distributed in the US and Canada by Octopus
Books USA
c/o Hachette Book Group USA
237 Park Avenue South, New York NY 10017

In the recipes all eggs are large unless
otherwise stated

A CIP catalogue record for this book is available
from the British Library.

ISBN 978 1 84533 524 3

Commissioning Editor: Rebecca Spry
Executive Art Editor: Yasia Williams
Designer: Miranda Harvey
Editor: Hattie Ellis
Photography: Jason Lowe
Home economy: Sunil Vijayakar
Production: Seyhan Essen
Index: John Noble
Americanization: Caitlin Doyle

Printed and bound by Toppan
Printing Company in China

Typeset in Formata and Garamond

For Iain, with all my love

Many people talked to me about the food of their homelands, fed me, and shared recipes while I was researching this book. It would have been impossible to write it without them. I would particularly like to thank the following: Johanna Oldroyd, Margareta Furlong, and Anna Mosesson for chatting endlessly about Swedish food; the chef and owners of the *Fryksas Hotel*, Orsa, Sweden; the chef and staff from the *Restaurant Wiinblad* at the *Hotel d'Angleterre* and the owners of *Grabrodre Torv* restaurant in Copenhagen; Kasia Szczawinska for her passion for Eastern European food; the chef and staff at *Les Roches Fleuries* in Cordon, Haute Savoie, France; Elena and Franco from *Pa'Krhaizar* in Sauris, Friuli, Italy; Doris and Alois Rottensteiner from *Patschieder Hof* near Bolzano and Karl Mair from *Pretzhof* in Val di Vizze, both in the Alto Adige, Italy; Esben Gregersen from the restaurant *Bryggen Tracteursted*, Anders and Sue Fretheim, Trond Moi, Edel Alpen, Anders Christensen from *Gamlavaerket* and all the other food-lovers I spent time with in Norway; the chef and staff at *Pirauer* and *Café Sperl* in Vienna. Thanks also goes to those who funded research travels and helped on the ground in various corners of the world. I am particularly grateful to the Norwegian Tourist Board and Sian Davies; Ocean Spray; Irene Sorenson and the cranberry growers of Cape Cod; Siobhan Meaker and Gerri McNally from Field McNally Leathes for a great time in Massachusetts; David and Jane Sandelman from the Weathersfield Inn, Ed Eagan and Jason Aldous for terrific hospitality in Vermont; Willis and Tina Wood, Catherine Stevens, and the sugar-makers of Vermont who were so patient and let me experience a sugar-on-snow party. Dawn Hayward, from the New England Culinary Institute and Johanna Tedone from Black River Produce in Proctorsville, Vermont, were stars who gave invaluable support and advice for the photo shoot.

Various people gave or allowed me to adapt particular recipes, so thanks to Rosie Stark, Desmond Millar, Philip and Karen Burgess from the Dartmoor Inn at Lydford, Devon, Hennickehammers Herrgard in Filipstad Sweden, *Café Sperl*, Vienna, John McClure and the *Baba a Louis* Bakery in Chester, Vermont, Alois Rottensteiner from Patscheider Hof, Bolzano, Italy.

The usual team of Hattie Ellis, editor, Becca Spry, commissioning editor, and Miranda Harvey, designer, made work, once again, stimulating, fulfilling, and a great laugh. Jason Lowe's photographs are wonderfully original, as ever, and Sunil Vijayakar and Rebecca Faill did a sterling job cooking on the shoot. Thanks also to Yasia Williams and Tim Foster for overseeing the design and to Samantha Lierens who did a fantastic job clearing copyrights.

A special mention must go to Martha Munro, an extraordinary teacher and the person who introduced me to the joys of Laura Ingalls Wilder's *Little House* books and therefore "sugar snow".

The biggest thanks, as ever, goes to my husband, Iain, and my son, Ted, who did most of the travel and research with me and survived many meals, extreme cold, being snowed in, and even a serious altercation with an Italian snowplow. You were both great.

Grateful acknowledgment is made for permission to reprint excerpts from the following previously published works: extract from *Little House in the Big Woods* by Laura Ingalls Wilder, text copyright 1932, 1960 Little House Heritage Trust, used by Permission of HarperCollins Publishers – "LITTLE HOUSE" ® is a registered trademark of HarperCollins Publishers Inc; *Figs* from *The Complete Poems* of D.H. Lawrence, reproduced by permission of Laurence Pollinger Ltd and the Estate of Frieda Lawrence Ravagli; *Pilgrim at Tinker Creek* by Annie Dillard, reproduced by permission of Macmillan Ltd; *Blackberry Picking* from *Death of a Naturalist* by Seamus Heaney and *The Fish* by Marianne Moore from *The Complete Poems*, reproduced by permission of Faber and Faber Ltd; *A Legacy* by Sybille Bedford, Copyright © Sybille Bedford, 1964, and *Embers* by Sandor Marai, translated by Carol Brown Janeway, Copyright © Heirs of Sandor Marai, Vorosvary-Weller Publishing, Toronto, reproduced by permission of Penguin Books; *Heartburn* by Nora Ephron, published by Virago, reproduced by kind permission of the author; *Blue Trout and Black Truffles* by Joseph Wechsberg, reproduced by permission of Academy Chicago Publishers; *Playing Sardines* by Michele Roberts, Copyright © Michele Roberts 2001, reproduced by permission of Gillon Aitken Associates; *A Kipper with my Tea* by Alan Davidson, reproduced by kind permission of the author's estate and Macmillan Ltd; *Black Pudding* by John Fuller, reproduced by kind permission of the author and Secker and Warburg; *An Ode to English Food* from **Collected Poems 1958-1982** by George Macbeth, Copyright © George Macbeth 1989, published by Hutchinson, reproduced by permission of Sheil Land Associates Ltd; *Wild Fruits* by Henry David Thoreau, edited by Bradley P. Dean, Copyright © 2000 Bradley P. Dean, reproduced by permission of W.W. Norton & Company, Inc; *The Accidental Tourist* by Anne Tyler, published by Chatto and Windus, *Cider with Rosie* by Laurie Lee, published by Chatto and Windus, *After Apple Picking*, *In a Glass of Cider* and *Evening in a Sugar Orchard* from *The Poetry of Robert Frost* edited by Edward Connery Lathem, published by Jonathan Cape, all reproduced by permission of The Random House Group Ltd; *This is just to say*, by William Carlos Williams, from *The Collected Poems of W.C. Williams, Vol.2, 1909-1939*, edited by Christopher McGowan (1945) reproduced by permission of Carcanet Press Ltd; *Earthly Paradise*, writings of Colette selected by Robert Phelps, reproduced by the Estate of Colette and Farrar, Straus & Giroux; the foreword to *Sugartime* by Susan Carol Hauser, foreword by William Weaver, reproduced by permission of Lyons Press; *Memories of Gascony* by Pierre Koffmann, reproduced by permission of Hamlyn; *Mr. Palomar* by Italo Calvino, reproduced by permission of The Random House Group Ltd; *Little House in the Big Woods* by Laura Ingalls Wilder, reproduced by permission of HarperCollins; *Black Earth City*, by Charlotte Hobson, published by Granta, reproduced by permission of A.P. Watt on behalf of the author; poetry by R.S. Thomas reprinted with permission of Orion Publishing Group.

The author and publisher apologize for any errors or omissions in the above list and would be grateful to be notified of any corrections that should be incorporated in a reprint.

CONTENTS

INTRODUCTION

For me, food is as much to do with the imagination as it is with flavor. A dish is more than a collection of ingredients. It comes from somewhere, contains tastes that make you think of the sun or snow, and may be a classic of home-cooking prepared every day in some corner of the world. In short, food comes with associations, with history, and it can take us places.

My first book, *Crazy Water, Pickled Lemons*, was about the enchantment of ingredients from the Middle East and Mediterranean—pomegranates, dates, saffron, olives—and how exotic I had found them as I was growing up under a cold gray northern Irish sky. My interest was fueled by stories such as *The Arabian Nights*, and *Roast Figs, Sugar Snow* has also been inspired by childhood reading, though of books set in a very different world. On dark afternoons, my high-school teacher read us the stories of Laura Ingalls Wilder. In the simple snowy world of the American Midwest found in *Little House in the Big Woods*, an orange and a handful of nuts in the toe of a sock on Christmas Day seemed as alluring as the seeds from a crimson pomegranate; fat pumpkins gathered in the fall and stored in the attic were fairy-tale vegetables. But it was the story of maple syrup that intrigued me most: how you could tap the sap of maple trees when there was a "sugar snow" (snowy conditions in which the temperature goes below freezing at night but above freezing during the day), boil the sap down to a sticky amber syrup, and pour it onto snow. There it set to a cobwebby toffee. Here was a magical food that you could get from inside a tree and make into candy. I got my first bottle of maple syrup soon after being read this passage and have loved it ever since.

This book isn't just about ingredients. It's also about the weather and seasons, and the kind of food we want to eat and cook in colder months. I've always enjoyed fall and winter cooking more than summer cooking. I like the way you gradually turn in on yourself as the weather cools. Life slows down and so does cooking. Cold-weather dishes undergo slow transformations: alchemy takes place as meat and root vegetables, through careful handling and gentle heat, become an unctuous stew, a dish far greater than the sum of its parts. The techniques employed in the kitchen fug the windows and seal you in, and you find you want different foods. You can't argue with your body as it craves potatoes and pulses: the winter appetite is about survival.

Even without their cooking, fall and winter are my favorite seasons. Perhaps it is the result of growing up in Northern Ireland. I find comfort in drizzle and beauty in hueless skies just as much as in the colors of fall foliage and the smokiness of autumnal air. And I adore snow—its crystalline freshness, the silent mesmeric way it falls, the way it blankets you in a white, self-contained world. I don't ski, but every winter I set off for some white region to go walking. For a long time I went to the Haute Savoie, where I fell in love with the food: dishes based on molten cheese, game, apples, pears, and nuts. Curiosity about cold-weather flavors took hold of me and I decided to explore other cold places.

In Russia, I found pork served with pickled apples, game birds with beets, and sour cream and curd cheese pancakes with roast plums. (Russian literature is full of food—Solzhenitsyn wrote that prisoners in the Gulag desperately wanted to get their hands on books by Gogol and Chekhov, but when they did it was almost unbearable because the descriptions of food were so vivid.) I visited Austria, Switzerland, Hungary, Scandinavia, Northern Italy, America, and other areas of France, collecting recipes as I went, and soon realized what a great hunting ground these countries are for a British cook. They all use much the same basic fall and winter produce as we do—root vegetables and brassicas, orchard fruits, pork, game, and cheese—but their flavor combinations are different. These trips have had a profound effect on my cooking. The dill in Scandinavia brings a breath of chill air and pine forests to the table; the pairing of horseradish with pork, as in Austria and Russia, makes you see the potential of a root we only bring out for roast beef; peppers and tomatoes cooked with blood-red paprika produces a Hungarian ratatouille that is more suited to winter consumption than the Mediterranean version.

While roasting as many Mediterranean vegetables as the next person, I worry about what the "Mediterraneanisation" of cooking is doing to the native home-cooking of many countries. It was thrilling to find that, despite the inroads made by this trend, and by "fusion" cooking, there is plenty of traditional home-cooking going on that doesn't appear to be under threat. The Valle d'Aosta in northwest Italy offers soups thick with rye bread, venison braised with spices, and orchard fruits cooked in wine, while the Alto Adige region in the northeast has oversized dumplings made with beets, and buckwheat cakes filled with berries. Snowed in one Christmas in Friuli, in the far northeast of Italy, I huddled round innumerable *fogolars* —the big hearths in the center of every Friulian home and inn—and enjoyed sweet-sour salads of magenta treviso and squash gnocchi showered with crumbs of smoked ricotta, goulash of beef cheeks, and apple strudel.

Time and again I found food like this, food that is unique to its area and impossible to find elsewhere. Perhaps the body's natural need for solid food in cold weather, coupled with the geographical separateness of mountain regions, has ensured the longevity of traditional dishes in such places. Snow and mountains seem to create and preserve a way of life and a way of eating.

Much of the food I found has romance too, just as Middle Eastern dishes have. A cake rich with poppy seeds makes you think of Magyars, dancing bears, and richly embroidered gypsy dresses; many Scandinavian dishes, such as their Christmas rice pudding, studded with almonds and berries, or their heart-shaped ginger biscuits, are pure fairy tale, linking modern Scandinavians with their countryside and their past.

The Scandinavians seem to be much better at dealing with cold dark months than we are. The Danes in particular get great succour from food in the fall and winter. Hunkering down in a café filled with candlelight to eat a cardamom-scented pastry with a big mug of coffee is what they describe as "*hygge*", an untranslatable term meaning: "cozy, warming, life-affirming". The idea that winter food is drab and brown is misplaced. Food is the Scandinavian antidote to darkness. I hope the dishes in here will become yours.

> *"Behind every cheese there is a different pasture of a different green under a different sky."*
>
> MR. PALOMAR ITALO CALVINO

RIPE AND READY
cheese

I cannot imagine a day without cheese. Tangy Cheddar melting on toast, a hunk of nutty Beaufort with an apple and a green salad, a piece of creamy Cashel Blue with a couple of honey-grilled figs. This is the kind of food I lunch on every day. You never tire of cheese; there is always another one to try or a new dish to cook with a familiar cheese. Cheesemaking may be simple in theory—a starter culture makes milk coagulate into curds, which are then pressed—but think of the textures and flavors on offer: a precipice of sweet, crumbling Parmesan; a ripe, snowy Camembert, its insides full to bursting; Epoisses, pungent and supple with an orangey rind that sticks to your fingers. These differences are the result of all the variables that can affect a cheese: what milk is used, whether the animal has grazed on grass or hay, and whether the ground is clay or limestone, volcanic or granite. The way the cheese coagulates and the curds are cut and pressed, the salting method used, the length and place of curing, all have a bearing on the final cheese, too. It's amazing to think most cheeses are the result of centuries of farmers and dairymen playing with chance, imagination, and their taste buds. And it all comes from one simple ingredient, milk, the primal food of every mammal.

Cheese is one of the best cold-weather foods, and some cheeses, such as the Swiss Vacherin Mont d'Or, which you can bake for half an hour in its wooden box and scoop up with little warm potatoes, are made for winter. Cooked, cheese becomes melting, warm, and creamy, giving both comfort and central heating to our bodies, and there are some great classic wintry cheese dishes. For years I stayed every winter in a little family-run hotel in the Haute Savoie. Here the cheese board was the crowning glory of every meal. "*Vous avez choisi, Madame?*" the owner would ask me every night. He knew that, faced with two tiers of cheeses from the Savoie and the Jura in peak condition, I didn't want to choose at all—I wanted the whole damned lot. Even better, the restaurant here showed me that the joys of cooked Alpine cheeses weren't limited to fondue. *Tartiflette,* a Savoyard dish of potatoes and onions topped with a creamy blanket of melting Reblochon, is one of the most satisfying dishes I know. Add the traditional accompaniments of salami, little sweet-and-sour onions, *cornichons,* and a green salad and you wonder why you ever bother to cook anything fancier. Then there's pumpkin or onion soup smothered in molten Gruyère, and Raclette, an ancient mountain cheese made in the French Savoie and the Valais region of Switzerland. Once heated on a grill, it becomes sweetly savory and wonderfully elastic, perfect for scooping up with bread or potatoes.

In the Italian Dolomites, you find pasta with pumpkin and nuggets of smoked ricotta, and in Italy's Valle d'Aosta, there is a soup made up of layers of bread, greens, and supple fontina, all collapsing in the warmth of chicken broth. Away from the ski slopes in the cold of a Normandy winter, you find Camembert soaked in Calvados and baked. Alsace offers little toasts covered with melting spicy Munster and served with plum compote or toasted cumin seeds, and Piedmont has risottos so dripping with Taleggio that they practically have to be eaten with a spoon. Britain has Welsh rarebit, tarts stuffed with smoked fish and mature Cheddar, and deep bowls of cauliflower soup scattered with salty Stilton. In these dishes, cheese is the undisputed star, but there are plenty of others in which it is the enhancer, blending well with another distinct ingredient: pork chops topped with a layer of ham and Gruyère cheese; a rare steak dotted with piquant Roquefort butter; or a gratin of haddock, mussels, and spinach baked with Cheddar.

But you don't have to cook much to make cheese into a lunch or supper. Want an effortless end to a wintry meal instead of making a dessert? Serve damson or quince cheese with a wedge of Stilton or Lanark Blue; pair Gorgonzola and mascarpone with drizzles of honey and freshly shelled walnuts, or with pears poached in spiced red wine; or offer vintage apples with a hunk of Montgomery Cheddar and freshly picked cobnuts.

Some cheeses—Cheddar, Gorgonzola, and Camembert, for example—seem right for eating all year round, but there are others with a particularly wintry appeal. Those from the French, Swiss, and Italian Alps, not surprisingly, hit the spot. Put the Savoyard Beaufort at the top of your list. Floral and milkily nutty, this is the supreme Gruyère-type cheese and worth more than just grating into a fondue. Other good elastic melting cheeses, though all of them less aromatic than Beaufort, are Comté, Emmenthal, and Gruyère. Look out, also, for Tomme de Savoie, an ancient French mountain cheese made in the winter, with a gentle taste of meadows.

The semi-soft Morbier, from the Jura, is sweet and fruity with a yeasty smell and a layer of ash through the middle. It's such a good melter that a wheel of it would traditionally be set up near the fire and scraped off on to bread or hot potatoes as it started to soften. Reblochon, the one used to make *tartiflette*, is a semi-soft washed rind cheese with a farmyardy smell yet a taste of walnuts and flowers. Swiss Vacherin Mont d'Or, a gloriously fruity cheese, is so smooth and runny that it can be eaten with a spoon. Baked in its wooden box until the crust becomes golden, it makes a great meal for two; like a fondue but without the hassle. Taleggio, a great grilling cheese from Lombardy (try it over hot polenta), has a rusty-hued crust and a melting curd that smells of almonds and hay. Fontina, a smooth elastic cheese from the Valle d'Aosta, tastes of mushrooms and is used for the Italian-style fondue dish, *fonduta*. Blue cheeses are great with fall fruits, nuts, and bitter winter leaves such as chicory—try dense Fourme d'Ambert from the Auvergne in southwest France, or the mild Bleu du Haut Jura (also known as Bleu de Gex) as well as clean, crumbly Roquefort.

Sadly, too many Scandinavian cheeses are made by big cooperatives rather than small artisans, but it's worth searching out the Swedish Herrgårdsost—fresh, tangy, nutty, and Gruyère-like—and Danish Samsø, with its tiny holes and pungent sweet-sour flavor. Norwegian Gjetost, a really sweet cheese made from whey, is delicious with pickles and ham and is often used to make a sauce to go with game, especially venison. It's not to everyone's taste—when I say it's fudgy I mean it—but it's distinctive and everyone should try it once.

All this makes cheese shopping—trying to choose between all those turrets and wheels and neat little boxes—one of the most pleasurable activities I know. Use the cold months to track down a good cheese shore and see what the snowy regions of the world have to offer.

When I was testing this recipe—a soup from the Valle d'Aosta in northern Italy—my friend Daniel, an ex-ski instructor, happened to turn up and he devoured the lot. There's nothing like this soup for making your house smell like a ski chalet.

I veer from the traditional version by adding the cabbage only for the last 15 minutes, because traditionally you cook the cabbage in butter and layer it up with everything else before baking, so do that if you prefer to stick to the authentic version; I just like it fresher. Use more or less bread, depending on how thick you want your soup to be.

ZUPPA ALLA VALPELLEUNENZE

serves 6

3 tbsp butter

4 garlic cloves, finely sliced

12oz (350g) rye or coarse country bread, or a mixture of the two, torn into chunks about 2½ inches (3cm) square

10½oz (300g) fontina, thinly sliced

salt and pepper

6 cups chicken stock

1lb 5oz (600g) Savoy cabbage, shredded

2 tbsp grated Parmesan

1 Preheat the oven to 310°F (160°C). Melt 1oz (30g) of the butter and gently sauté the garlic, without coloring. Layer the bread and fontina in a casserole dish, adding the garlic, garlicky butter, and seasoning with salt and pepper as you go. Heat the chicken stock and pour it over the layers. Put in the preheated oven for 45 minutes.

2 Melt the rest of the butter in a heavy-bottomed pan and add the cabbage with a couple of tablespoons of water, and some salt and pepper. Turn the heat down low, cover the pan, and cook the cabbage for about 4 minutes, shaking it vigorously every so often.

3 Take the casserole out of the oven and turn the heat up to 350°F (180°C). Stir the cabbage with its buttery juices into the baked soup. Sprinkle with the Parmesan and put back into the oven for a further 15 minutes. Serve immediately.

French onion soup, Normandy-style. Have a Kleenex ready—there's nothing quite like it for unblocking the sinuses!

ONION AND CIDER SOUP
with melting Camembert

serves 8

½ cup (1 stick) butter

3lb 5oz (1.5kg) onions, very finely sliced

1 tbsp sugar (optional)

1 cup apple cider

4 cups chicken stock

leaves from 3 sprigs fresh thyme

8 slices bread from a baguette, toasted

1 Camembert

1 tbsp butter, melted

1 Melt the butter in a heavy-bottomed saucepan and add the onions. Sauté them gently, turning them around in the butter, until they start to soften. Add a splash of water, cover with a lid, and sweat the onions until they are very soft and starting to caramelize. This can take up to 50 minutes. You will need to add a splash of water every so often and turn the onions over in the buttery juices.

2 Take the lid off and turn the heat up to medium so that the juices can evaporate and the onions can caramelize. I often end up adding the sugar after a while if it is not caramelizing well, but sometimes, if the onions have a lot of their own sugar, you don't need to.

3 When the onions are dark, add the cider, stock, and thyme and bring to the boil. Simmer for 10 minutes.

4 Ladle the soup into 8 heavy bowls that won't crack under a high heat. Put a slice or two of toast on each bowl of soup. Cut the Camembert into slices and lay them on top. Brush with melted butter and heat under the grill until golden and bubbling. Serve immediately.

"If I had a son who was ready to marry, I would tell him, 'Beware of girls who don't like wine, truffles, cheese, or music.'"
EARTHLY PARADISE COLETTE

"*It seemed I was a* mite of sediment
    That waited for the bottom to ferment
    So I could catch a bubble in ascent.
    I rode up on one till the bubble burst,
    And when that left me to sink back reversed
    I was no worse off than I was at first.
    I'd catch another bubble if I waited.
    The thing was to get now and then elated."

IN A GLASS OF CIDER ROBERT FROST

Alsace's answer to pizza. You can add grated Gruyère or Munster cheese, though it's not traditional. This is usually served in big squares on wooden boards and then cut into individual slices, so do it that way if you prefer.

ALSATIAN TARTE FLAMBÉE

serves 4

⅛ cup dried yeast

2 cups lukewarm water

4 cups bread flour

1½ tsp salt

for the topping:

4½oz (125g) ricotta

4½oz (125g) cream cheese

good squeeze of lemon juice

1 cup sour cream

salt and pepper

2 tbsp oil, such as sunflower or a light-tasting olive oil

2 medium onions, very finely sliced

12oz (350g) smoked bacon lardons

I Begin by sponging the yeast. Dissolve the yeast in 1½ tbsp of the lukewarm water and mix with 2 tbsp of the flour. Stir everything together to make a smooth paste and leave to bubble under a cloth, somewhere warm, for 30 minutes.

2 Put about 3½ cups of the flour into a bowl and make a well in the center (save the rest for kneading). Pour the sponge, salt, and the rest of the water into the middle and mix, gradually bringing the dry ingredients into the liquid. Bring it all together so that it forms a ball. Then, with well-floured hands, knead the dough for 10 minutes until it is smooth, satiny, and elastic. Put in a clean bowl, cover loosely with a cloth, and leave somewhere warm to rise for 1½ hours, or until the dough has doubled in size.

3 Preheat the oven to 475°F (240°C), or as hot as you can get it. If using baking trays, lightly oil them using a wad of paper towel before you put the *tarte flambées* on to them. Put pizza stones, unglazed quarry or terra-cotta tiles, or baking trays into the oven.

4 Once the dough has risen, knock it back and roll it out into 4 rounds, about 9 inches (23cm) across. Mix the ricotta and cream cheese with the lemon juice then stir in the sour cream, seasoning, and oil and spread it over the top of each round. Sprinkle the onions and the bacon on top of this.

5 Transfer the tartes flambées onto the hot pizza stones, tiles, or baking trays in the preheated oven. Cook for about 15 minutes, until golden.

I first visited Russia when it was still under Communism and good eating opportunities were thin on the ground. In Leningrad we lunched every day in a basement canteen, eating fatty dumplings, filled either with jam or sausage, and sickly sweet tea. Supper was cabbage, tinned ham, and cherryade. In Moscow, however, I discovered the delights of Georgian food and have loved it ever since, as do the Russians themselves. We drove through what seemed like miles of gray concrete blocks to reach the restaurant. An anonymous door led into a wood-panelled room pulsating with gypsy music and a clientele made up of the grandees of Russian society—ballet dancers, musicians, and politicians—where we were served *zakuski*, a spread of Russian appetizers. These cheese pies were the best things on offer, enhanced by beans in plum sauce, beet and walnut purée, radishes, and all the other things that form part of the splendid *zakuski* spread. For other *zakuski* recipes, see pages 152–154.

GEORGIAN CHEESE PIES

serving 4 as a snack
makes 2 x 9 inch (23cm) pies

2½ cups bread flour

1 cup Greek yogurt

2 tbsp milk

½ tsp salt

1 tsp baking powder

for the filling:

8oz (225g) mozzarella, cut into small chunks

4oz (115g) feta, crumbled

2 tbsp Greek yogurt

pepper

2 small eggs, beaten

2 tbsp butter, melted

I Preheat the oven to 350°F (180°C). Make the dough by sifting the flour and then mixing in the other ingredients. Add more flour if you need to—the dough should be soft but not sticky. Knead until smooth and elastic. Divide the dough into 4 equal pieces, then roll them into circles of approximately 9 inches (23cm) with 2 just slightly bigger than the other 2. Put the slightly larger circles on 2 buttered baking trays.

2 Mix all the filling ingredients together and divide it between the 2 larger circles of dough, leaving an edge of about 1 inch (2.5cm). Dampen the edges of the dough with water, then lay the slightly smaller circles on top. Fold the edge of the larger base circle over the top circle of dough. Brush with the melted butter and bake in the preheated oven for 25 minutes. Serve hot, cut into squares or wedges.

For years I went every winter to the same little hotel in a village in the French Savoie, about half an hour from Chamonix. Apart from the snow and the view of Mont Blanc, the real pull in this place was their tiny restaurant, La Boîte aux Fromages. Every night we ate eat simple Savoyard specialities—salads of Gruyère and cured ham, creamy gratins of *crozets* (buckwheat pasta), served with veal chops, and thick sausages braised with potatoes: pure mountain food. This was my favorite dish. It is traditionally made with French Reblochon cheese, but as it's now illegal to import it into the USA try another washed-rind cheese such as Gres des Vosges. You can leave the bacon out if you want to make a vegetarian version. Either way, a plain green salad is a good foil for the richness.

TARTIFLETTE

serves 6

3lb (1.3kg) waxy potatoes, (no need to peel)

salt and pepper

3 tbsp unsalted butter

2 tbsp olive oil

9oz (250g) chunky bacon lardons

1 onion, roughly chopped

2 garlic cloves, crushed

12oz (350g) washed-rind cheese, such as Gres de Vosges

½ cup crème fraîche

1 Cook the potatoes in boiling salted water until just tender. Drain. When they are cool enough to handle, slice the potatoes. Heat half the butter and oil together in a frying pan and cook the potatoes until they are golden. Season with salt and pepper and put them into a shallow ovenproof dish.

2 Preheat the oven to 375°F (190°C). Heat the rest of the butter and oil in the same frying pan and cook the lardons over a fairly high heat to color them well. Turn the heat down, add the onion, and cook it until soft and just beginning to colour. Throw in the garlic and cook for another couple of minutes. Add this to the ovenproof dish and gently combine with the potatoes.

3 Cut the cheese into slices and trim the rind. Dot spoonfuls of crème fraîche all over the potatoes and cover with the slices of chseese. Bake in the preheated oven for 15 minutes. The cheese should be melted and bubbling. Serve immediately.

Eaten in Piedmont and the Valle d'Aosta in northern Italy, this risotto is so rich with melting fontina that it can practically be eaten with a spoon. If you have some meat or chicken juices, stir them in at the end. Sliced white truffles can be sprinkled on top should you be lucky enough to have any.

ANTICO RISOTTO SABAUDO

serves 4–6

4 tbsp butter

1 medium onion, finely chopped

4¼ cups chicken stock

3oz (75g) good-quality cooked ham, cut into chunks about ¾ inch (2cm) square

4 cups arborio rice

leaves from 1 sprig rosemary, chopped

¾ cup dry white wine

4½oz (125g) fontina, cut into about 1-inch (2.5-cm) cubes

2 tbsp freshly grated Parmesan

pepper

1 Melt the butter in a heavy-bottomed pan and sauté the onion until soft but not colored. Bring the stock up to simmering point. Add the ham to the onion and cook for another minute, then stir the rice and rosemary around in the buttery juices for about a minute, or until the rice is transparent.

2 Add the wine, stir, and cook until the wine has been absorbed. Start adding the simmering stock, a ladleful at a time, adding the next ladleful only when the previous one has been absorbed. You need to stir continuously. After about 20 minutes the rice should be soft and creamy but retain a little "bite". Stir in the fontina and cook for another 5 minutes, stirring.

3 Stir in the Parmesan and taste—it probably won't need any seasoning, particularly salt because of the cheeses and stock, but just make sure. Serve immediately.

I've had versions of this delicious, old-fashioned dish in the Alps of Switzerland and France, and there are Italian versions as well. It's rich, so it's best to eat it at the end of a day of hard physical activity! Use Gruyère if you can't get hold of Beaufort and serve with a green salad and thick buttered noodles.

POULET SUISSESSE

serves 6

6 chicken breast joints, bone-in, skin-on

2 tbsp unsalted butter

2 tbsp olive oil

1 cup white wine

salt and pepper

⅛ cup breadcrumbs

for the sauce:

4 tbsp butter

½ cup all-purpose flour

whole milk

⅓ cup crème fraîche

1½ tsp Dijon mustard

good grating nutmeg

1½oz (40g) Parmesan, grated

4½oz (125g) Beaufort or Gruyère cheese, grated

1 Heat the butter and oil together in a frying pan and quickly brown the chicken pieces all over. You want to get a good color, not to cook the chicken through. Drain off the excess fat from the pan and pour on the white wine. Scrape the bottom of the pan with a wooden spoon to dislodge all the crusty cooking juices. Season with salt and pepper. Bring the wine to just under the boil, then turn down the heat, cover the pan, and cook the chicken on a gentle simmer for 15 minutes.

2 Preheat the oven to 350°F (180°C). Remove the chicken and set it aside. Pour the juices into a pitcher. Make a roux by melting the butter in the frying pan and adding the flour. Stir this over a medium heat until the butter and flour blend and turn a pale brown. Remove the pan from the heat. Measure the juices from the chicken and add enough milk to make 19fl oz (550ml) of liquid. Start adding this to the roux, a little at a time, stirring to incorporate each addition. When all the liquid has been added, put the pan back on the heat and bring to the boil, stirring all the time until the sauce thickens. Add the crème fraîche and let the sauce simmer for 5 minutes to cook out the flour, then add the mustard, nutmeg, salt and pepper, and cheeses, keeping back ½oz (15g) of the Parmesan to scatter over the top. Cook for a few more minutes until the cheeses have melted, but don't overcook, as melted cheese can become very oily. Add any of the juices that have leached out of the chicken and taste for seasoning.

3 Put the chicken into an ovenproof gratin dish and pour the sauce over it. Scatter the breadcrumbs and reserved Parmesan on top and bake in the preheated oven for 20 minutes. Flash the dish under the grill until the top is golden-brown and bubbling and serve.

My pancake love started 15 years ago, when Patricia Wells' book *Food Lovers' Guide to France* led me to the Café des Artisans, a little *crêperie* on a cobbled street in Dinan, Brittany. Here I sampled my first *galettes de sarrasin*: dark, nutty-tasting buckwheat crêpes. Surrounded by dusty accordions, old advertising posters, and bottles of alcoholic cider, I perused the café's single-sheet menu. I expected to find buckwheat crêpes with smoked salmon and cream, but I wasn't planning on finding mushrooms, walnuts, and Roquefort, or sausage, bacon, and potatoes in a mustard sauce: it seems that almost anything can go into a buckwheat crêpe. French cider is the obvious accompaniment, drunk, Breton style, out of large teacups.

GALETTES SOUBISES

serves 6

1¼ cups all-purpose flour

1¼ cups buckwheat flour

1 tsp salt

1¼ cups milk

½ cup water

2 large eggs

2 tbsp butter, melted

flavorless oil, such as peanut or sunflower

for the filling:

½ cup (1 stick) butter

2 large onions, very finely chopped

3 tbsp heavy cream

salt and pepper

1lb (450g) smoked bacon lardons

4½oz (125g) Gruyère or Emmenthal, grated

6 large eggs

1 Sift the flours and salt into a large bowl and make a well in the center. Beat together the milk, water, and eggs in a bowl and gradually pour into the well, whisking the flour into it as you go. Stir in the melted butter and let the batter sit.

2 For the filling, melt the butter in a saucepan and sweat the onions over a very low heat. You may need to add a splash of water to stop them from sticking to the bottom of the pan—the onions must not color, but should soften (about 20 minutes). Add the cream, season with salt and pepper, and set aside. Sauté the bacon in its own fat until golden and keep warm.

3 To cook the *galettes*, heat a tiny bit of oil in a large frying pan. Add half a ladleful of the batter and swirl it around the pan so that it reaches all the sides. The batter for these is thicker than normal crêpe batter, so you have to really swirl it to get it to move. Cook until brown and set underneath, then flip the pancake over with a spatula and cook the other side. Add a little more oil for each pancake.

4 You can either cover the pancake with the various components of the filling—bacon, onions, and cheese—and then break an egg on top and let it cook on the pancake, or you can fry the egg separately. To be honest, I never find it easy to get the egg to cook on the pancake. I usually add the other fillings, let the cheese melt as the *galette* finishes cooking, and fry the eggs in a separate pan, adding them at the end. In France they fold the pancakes over, but I think they look best open, so that you can see the filling.

Stuffed baked potatoes are even more of a treat than a plain baked potato. These cheese-rich ones are from Normandy, so have them with a glass of French cider. Use a thick slice of good baked ham, cut for you at the butchers or at the deli counter.

POMMES DE TERRE BRAYTOISES

serves 4

4 large potatoes

¼ cup (½ stick) butter

salt and pepper

9oz (250g) Camembert

4oz (115g) cooked ham, cut into small chunks (about 1½ inch/4cm square)

8 tbsp crème fraîche

2 tsp Dijon mustard

1 small egg

4½oz (125g) Gruyère, grated

I Make small incisions in the potatoes and bake them in an oven preheated to 400°F (200°C) for 50 minutes to 1 hour, or until tender. Cut the potatoes in half and carefully scoop out the flesh, leaving the skin intact. Mash the flesh with the butter and season well with salt and pepper. Reduce the oven temperature to 350°F (180°C).

2 Cut away the rind from the Camembert and mix the rest of the cheese with the mashed potato, ham, 3 tbsp of the crème fraîche, mustard, and egg. Mash together and check the seasoning.

3 Divide the mixture between the 8 potato skins. Put the rest of the crème fraîche and the Gruyère on top of each potato. Bake the filled potatoes for 10 minutes in the now-cooler oven, then quickly flash under a hot grill until the tops of the potatoes are golden and bubbling.

4 Serve with a green salad, or a salad of watercress and walnuts dressed with a walnut vinaigrette.

*"Baked potatoes had always been their favorite food...
He thought back on years and years of winter
evenings: the kitchen windows black outside, the
corner furry with gathering darkness, the four of
them seated at the chipped enamel table meticulously
filling scooped-out potato skins with butter."*

THE ACCIDENTAL TOURIST ANNE TYLER

Fondue sets are more likely to be an unwanted wedding gift, stuck at the back of a cupboard, than a piece of much-loved kitchen paraphernalia but they are making a comeback according to style journalists. For me, they were never out. I can't think of a better cold-weather dinner than bread dipped in molten cheese, and you don't need any fancy equipment: you can make a fondue for two in a saucepan on a very low flame on the stove and eat it right beside the stove. Cubes of rustic bread are the traditional dippers, and I like *charcuterie* and pickled gherkins on the side and a fruity, spicy white wine such as a Riesling. The key thing is not to let your fondue boil.

FONDUE SAVOYARD

serves 2

4½oz (125g) each of Beaufort, Gruyère, and Raclette

light grating of fresh nutmeg

¼ garlic clove, crushed

1 cup hard cider or fruity white wine

salt and white pepper

dash of Calvados

I Coarsely grate the 3 cheeses, add the nutmeg, garlic, and a little of the cider and let everything sit together for about an hour before cooking. This soaking helps make a smoother fondue.

2 Bring the rest of the cider up to the boil in a heavy-bottomed pan or fondue pan, turn the heat down low, and add the cheese mixture. Stir in a figure-of-eight motion—this helps maintain a smooth consistency and prevents separation—until well blended and the consistency of custard. Season with salt and white pepper and add a splash of Calvados. Serve with cubes of lightly toasted rustic bread.

"We may, indeed, divide cheeses into two groups, the romantic and the classic. They are very easily distinguished. The romantics are apt to run over and become a little offensive when over-ripe. Classic cheeses do not; age may set them a little more firmly, but they never give way to it. Pungency and sting they may and do have, but all within the limits of decency."

THE EPICURE'S COMPANION EDWARD BUNYARD

This dish, which I've been cooking for years, is from my friend and fellow food writer, Rosie Stark. It's fabulous with venison or pork sausages and, with the charred spring onions on top, looks like a real feast and not just a bowl of mash. Use a mashing potato such as White Rose, Yukon Gold, or Red Rose. The dish is fine made in advance and gently reheated—just add a little milk to loosen it.

CELERIAC AND POTATO MASH
with Stilton and grilled scallions

serves 8

2 large heads celeriac

2 large potatoes

⅓ cup whole milk

⅓ cup (5⅓ tbsp) butter

4 tbsp heavy cream

salt and pepper

freshly grated nutmeg, to taste (optional)

4oz (115g) Stilton, crumbled

16 scallions, trimmed

olive oil

1 Peel both the celeriac and the potatoes. Cut the celeriac into chunks. Cook the 2 vegetables separately in salted water until they are tender. Drain both saucepans, mix the vegetables together in a saucepan, put a clean dish towel on top of them, and cover with the lid. Put the pan over a very low heat—this just helps the vegetables dry out a little and gives you a better textured mash.

2 Mash the vegetables and heat the milk. Add the hot milk, stirring as you do so, the butter and cream, and season with salt and pepper. I also like a good dose of nutmeg, but add it to your taste. Finally, add the Stilton—some of it should be well incorporated into the mash, some melting on the top. Cover to keep warm and quickly brush the scallions with oil. Cook them on a griddle pan, so that they get nice stripes, until they are just tender. Put the mash in a heated bowl, lay the green onions on top, and serve.

"So what else can I offer you? After these rather rich delicacies that we started with, how about a good, bitter salad of red chicory leaves, and perhaps a slice of Camembert served on a toothed chestnut leaf, and then a dish of pears poached in spices and red wine?"

THE COOKERY LESSON, PLAYING SARDINES MICHÈLE ROBERTS

These little pancakes, called *syrniki* in Russian, were the highlight of the breakfast spread in a big international hotel I once stayed in outside Moscow. They are delicious—feather-light and tangy—though better for dessert or brunch than regular breakfast, unless you're a bit of a pig.

RUSSIAN CHEESE PANCAKES
with plum compote

serves 6

1lb (450g) ricotta

1lb (450g) cream cheese

good squeeze of lemon

1 whole egg and 1 egg yolk

pinch salt

¼ cup superfine sugar

4–6 tbsp all-purpose flour

grated zest of ½ lemon

1 tsp vanilla extract

3 tbsp unsalted butter

for the plums:

1 cup red wine

1 cup water

⅔ cup superfine sugar

1 stick cinnamon

6 peppercorns, bruised

1 strip lemon peel

12oz (350g) plums

to serve:

confectioners sugar

sour cream

1 Mix the ricotta and cream cheese together with the lemon juice. If the mixture is wet, put it in some muslin and press it in a sieve with a wooden spoon (or let it drain over a bowl for several hours in the fridge) until it loses excess moisture. Mix with all the remaining ingredients, except the butter, and combine. Cover loosely with plastic wrap and chill for several hours then, using floured hands, form it into little flat cakes about 3½ inches (9cm) across. Put them on a floured baking tray, cover loosely again, and leave for another couple of hours, or until the following day.

2 To make the plum compote, put the wine, water, and sugar into a saucepan that will hold all the plums as well, and slowly bring up to the boil, stirring from time to time to help the sugar dissolve. Add the cinnamon, peppercorns, and lemon peel and turn the heat down to a very gentle simmer.

3 Add the plums, cover with a lid, and let them cook until tender but still whole (they should not be falling apart). Carefully lift the plums out of the liquid with a slotted spoon and put them in a dish. Boil the cooking juices until they are reduced by about two-thirds. You should end up with a syrup. (Remember that the liquid will get thicker and more syrupy as it cools.) Let the syrup cool, then pour it over the plums, and chill until you want to serve them.

4 Melt some butter in a frying pan and fry the pancakes on both sides until golden, adding a little butter for each pancake. Plate the little pancakes, sprinkle with confectioners sugar, and serve with dollops of sour cream and plum compote on the side.

GATHERING IN
chestnuts, hazelnuts, walnuts, and pecans

One of the best ends to a meal I have ever had was a bowl of apples from my host's garden, a chunk of farmhouse Cheddar, and a pile of cobnuts, still in their furry casings. Every element had a "nutty" taste, and the cobnuts were sweet and milky, but it was the pureness of the ingredients and the fact that we were all bound together in the same activity, creating piles of husks and shells, that made this food so enjoyable. It's not always easy to convince people, but this is sometimes the best kind of food you can offer.

Most nuts are grown in warm areas but, as with spices and dried fruits, countries with colder climates have adopted them as emblems of the bounty of fall and the stores of winter. In Middle European coffee houses from Prague to Vienna, hazelnuts, chestnuts, and walnuts stud gâteaux and fill pastries, and in the US and every northern European country, nuts appear at Christmas, as dependable as the fat man in the red coat.

Hazelnuts are the most sweetly nutty of nuts. They are the sopranos—small, smooth, high-pitched—to the walnut's deep bass notes. A cake made with walnuts has an earthy quality that makes you feel warm and contented; the same cake made with hazelnuts feels more jaunty. Hazelnuts start off milky and juicy in early fall, and become sweet and almost toasty after months of ripeness. They're good in many recipes in which you might otherwise use walnuts: salads of smoked duck, with blue- and Gruyère-type cheeses, with apples and pears, in cakes, cookies, and ice creams. The Italians love them, but the French Savoie is the area I've found them most used. Here, pasta parcels are stuffed with hazelnuts and pumpkin, and trout are stuffed with hazelnuts and mushrooms. Hazelnuts are also stirred into ice creams and incorporated into shortbread and tarts.

Walnuts are the royalty of the nut world. This noble nut doesn't have the pale, aristocratic elegance of the almond, but it is the king, both in terms of its widespread use and in its deep, meaty flavor, which comes mainly from the tannin in its skin. If you can, catch some at the early "wet" stage, when they are creamily sweet, with a golden papery skin covering the two perfect halves of their coruscated kernel.

The walnut tree is held in particularly high esteem in the Dordogne in France. For peasant families, they were a dependable crop—an assurance of prosperity—and they are still one of the most important products of the region. In the past, autumnal evenings were spent on *l'énoisement*, or nut-shelling, when family members told stories and sang songs. It is said every bit of the walnut was used except the noise it makes as it is cracked.

Walnuts that were not kept for eating were mixed with water, heated, and pressed for their oil, as they still are. The cookery of the area is suffused with the flavor of walnuts: the oil is used to dress salads, though always in conjunction with a milder oil, as nut oil has a strong flavor; the nuts are scattered over lettuce leaves, pressed into sourdough bread slathered with Roquefort, and tossed with green beans. A *digestif* is made by infusing red wine, sugar, and *marc* with tender young walnut leaves, and a liqueur is made from macerating fresh walnuts in *eau de vie*—delicious as a flavouring for ice cream or drizzled over poached pears.

Georgians adore walnuts too, using them in dishes that seem bizarre to us but nevertheless work, and that have been adopted by Russian cooks. Georgians stuff fish with walnuts and pomegranate seeds and make sauces by pounding walnuts with pomegranate molasses and roasted red peppers, or cilantro and beets. If you are looking for unusual uses for the nut, Italy also boasts a few lesser-known sauces. *Salsa di avi*, made with ground walnuts, honey, and mustard moistened with stock, is served with boiled meats in Piedmont, and Ligurians make *salsa di noci*, a kind of walnut pesto.

The pecan, the nut of a variety of hickory tree, is as American as apple pie. American cookbooks are full of uses for them, particularly in stuffings, salads, tarts, and old-fashioned desserts such as buckles, cobblers, and slumps. Pecans may look like walnuts, apart from their skin, which is the color of red squirrels, but their flavor is much sweeter, reminiscent of the burned sugariness of maple syrup. Pecans, like maple syrup, seem to match well with coffee; each flavor enhances the other so a plate of pecan cookies or a wedge of pecan cake always goes down well with an afternoon brew.

Chestnuts, their polished mahogany bodies glowing through those prickly green coats, are so beautiful that you long to like them. But you have to venture further than partnering them with brussels sprouts for that to happen. My chestnut devotion developed when I started to cook chestnuts with meat. Try sticking them into a pan of sausages braised with green onions and prunes or putting them alongside a roast joint of pork and you'll see why I was converted. Now I love their subtle, haunting sweetness and fudgy texture. Vacuum-packed cooked chestnuts are a great standby, but nothing beats the woody taste of freshly roasted nuts. Pierce the skin and roast the nuts in the oven, with a few tablespoons of water, for 10 minutes. Remove the outer skins, then simmer the nuts in a mixture of water and oil until the inner skins start to come off. Scoop them up, wrap in a cloth, and, while still warm, rub to completely remove the skins.

Although they are now regarded as a luxury, chestnuts used to be the food of the poor, a staple for peasants in the non-grain producing areas of southwest France and parts of Italy. Wild chestnuts were used to make flour—the chestnut tree was often referred to in France as *l'arbre à pain*, or the "bread tree". In many regions, chestnuts are still regarded as everyday fare. In northern Italy you'll find them in countless risottos, stewed with venison and juniper berries, braised with lentils, and, the greatest revelation, in salads with cured pork and spicy sausage. The French use chestnuts for soups, stuffings, and vegetable dishes such as chestnut gratin. They can't get enough of them in central Europe either. The Hungarians are particularly chestnut crazy. Roasting chestnuts at home is not unusual there and chestnut purée seems to be as ubiquitous as paprika.

Nuts are ancient and the activity of eating them propels us back to age-old behavior. Most of us don't go foraging in the woods for them, but we at least rifle through bags of hazelnuts and walnuts each Christmas, cracking them one by one. They bring a sense of the outside into the home. Whether walnuts are being cracked to eat with Stilton and port after a traditional English dinner, or chestnuts are being roasted on a grill in Budapest, their effect will be the same: at their most unadulterated, nuts are perfect chill-out food.

This is also good topped with a dash of truffle oil—very musky and earthy. If you want to try that, leave out the cream.

CHESTNUT AND JERUSALEM ARTICHOKE SOUP

serves 6

2 tbsp butter

1 leek, trimmed and cut into rings

½ onion, roughly chopped

1lb 9oz (700g) Jerusalem artichokes (unpeeled is fine)

9oz (250g) cooked chestnuts

4 cups chicken stock

1 cup whole milk

salt and pepper

¼ cup heavy cream

I Melt the butter in a heavy-bottomed saucepan and add the leek and onion. Add a splash of water, cover with a lid, and sweat for about 15 minutes, until soft but not colored. Check every so often to see whether you need to add another splash of water.

2 Chop the artichokes roughly and add them to the pan. Cover and cook for another 10 minutes, stirring them around in the buttery juices. Add 3oz (75g) of the chestnuts and the stock or water, and season. Simmer for 10 minutes, until the artichokes are tender. Add the milk and cream and, when the soup is cool enough, purée it. Chop the rest of the chestnuts and add them to the soup. Heat through and serve.

In northeast Italy I came across lots of hearty but elegant winter salads based on *charcuterie* and nuts. Use treviso in place of radicchio, or perhaps a straight chicory or endive, depending on what you can find.

FRIULIAN WINTER SALAD

serves 4 as a main course

½ tbsp balsamic vinegar

¼ cup extra virgin olive oil

salt and pepper

8oz (225g) radicchio, watercress and chicory

4½oz (125g) cooked chestnuts

1½ tbsp peanut oil

5½oz (150g) Speck or smoked bacon or pancetta, in cubes of ¾ inch (2cm)

150g (5½oz) spicy Italian sausage, skinned and broken into chunks

1oz (30g) toasted walnuts

seeds from ½ pomegranate

I Make the dressing by whisking together the vinegar, olive oil, and seasoning. Tear the radicchio leaves into pieces and separate the chicory leaves. Put all the leaves into a wide shallow bowl. Halve the chestnuts and put to one side.

2 Heat 1 tbsp of groundnut oil in a frying pan and cook the Speck and sausage over a high heat until well-colored and cooked through. Throw them onto the leaves. Heat the remaining ½ tbsp of oil and sauté the chestnuts until hot. Season.

3 Add the cooked chestnuts, walnuts, and dressing to the salad and toss. Sprinkle the pomegranate seeds over the top and serve immediately. At the restaurant where I ate this they sometimes serve it with a fried egg on top instead of the pomegranate seeds.

The Irish cheese, Cashel Blue, is one of my favorites. It's a rich, creamy blue and I always think it tastes slightly of smoked bacon. If you can't get hold of it, use Roquefort, Gorgonzola, or even Dolcelatte instead. This dish is based on a classic French bistro salad, for which they generally don't sauté the pear or include roast onion, so go down that route if you're feeling lazy. Apples can be used instead of pears and walnuts instead of hazelnuts.

SALAD OF PEAR, HAZELNUTS, AND CASHEL BLUE CHEESE

serves 6

1 small red onion

olive oil

salt and pepper

3 pears (not too ripe)

2 tbsp unsalted butter

3oz (75g) hazelnuts, lightly toasted but not skinned, halved

5½oz (150g) salad leaves, a mixture of watercress, chicory leaves, and baby spinach

6oz (175g) Cashel Blue cheese, crumbled

for the dressing:

2½ tsp white wine vinegar

drop Dijon mustard

4 tbsp hazelnut oil

2 tbsp light olive oil

1 tsp superfine sugar (or to taste)

1 Preheat the oven to 350°F (180°C). Halve the red onion and cut it into crescent-shaped slices. Put into a small ovenproof dish, drizzle with olive oil and season with salt and pepper. Roast in the preheated oven for 20–30 minutes, or until soft with slightly caramelized tips. Keep warm.

2 Make the dressing by whisking together all the ingredients. Season.

3 Halve and core the pears, then cut them lengthways into slices ¼ inch (¾cm) thick. Melt the butter in a frying pan and quickly sauté the pear slices on each side until golden. Don't overcook them—they should still hold their shape.

4 Toss the salad leaves with the nuts, using most of the dressing, then divide this between 6 plates. Add the pear slices and the warm onion to each plate and scatter with the cheese. Drizzle each plate with the rest of the dressing and serve.

"*Rien n'est perdu dans la noix, sauf le bruit qu'elle fait en se cassant.*"
  "*Nothing is wasted in the nut, except the sound as it is cracked.*"

SAYING IN SOUTHWEST FRANCE

"It will not always be like this,
*   The air windless, a few last*
*   Leaves adding their decoration*
*   To the tree's shoulders, braiding the cuffs*
*   Of the boughs with gold:*
*   Let the mind take its photograph*
*   Of the bright scene, something to wear*
*   Against the heart in the long cold."*

A DAY IN AUTUMN R.S. THOMAS

Nothing takes me to southwest France like this dish. Most people probably don't think of the area, with its red-tiled roofs and burning summers, as a cold-weather place—but if you visit in November, when every day seems shrouded in gauze, the *phut* of shooting is in the air and walnuts are on the menu, you'll find yourself in autumnal heaven. This is one of the classic dishes of the region and easy to make. Make sure your walnuts aren't stale or rancid, as they are the key flavoring.

DUCK BREAST
with *aillade*

serves 4

4 duck breast filets

6 tbsp brandy

leaves from 2 sprigs fresh thyme

salt and pepper

for the *aillade*:

1¼oz (35g) garlic cloves

3oz (75g) shelled walnuts

⅔ cup walnut oil

1 tbsp finely chopped flat-leaf parsley

1 Make 3 neat slashes in the skin of each duck breast and a few small discreet cuts on the other side too. Rub the brandy, thyme, salt, and pepper into the breasts and let them sit, loosely covered, in the fridge.

2 For the *aillade*, pound together the garlic and walnuts, either in a mortar or in a food processor using the pulse button—you want a chunky mixture—slowly drizzling in the the oil until you have a thick sauce. Season and stir in the chopped parsley.

3 Preheat the oven to 400°F (200°C). In a frying pan over a high heat, brown the duck breasts on both sides, skin-side down first: the duck will brown in its own fat. Once the breasts are a good color, roast in the preheated oven for 7 minutes. Cover with tin foil and insulate (I put a couple of heavy dish towels on top) and leave to sit for 3–4 minutes. Either carve the breasts into thick neat slices or serve whole, with the *aillade* and some fresh watercress.

I think pancakes are just one of the best things about American cooking. These buttermilk pancakes are thick, light, and fluffy—and totally addictive. Serve them on Sunday mornings—and go on, bring them to the table in a mile-high pile as if you're running your own diner—complete with a big pot of steaming coffee.

MILE-HIGH BUTTERMILK PANCAKES
with date and pecan butter and maple syrup

makes 12 x 3-inch (7.5-cm) pancakes

2½ cups all-purpose flour

1½ tsp baking powder

good pinch salt

2 tbsp superfine sugar

2 cups buttermilk

½ cup (1 stick) butter, melted

3 large eggs, 2 of them separated

for the date and pecan butter:

¾ cup (1½ sticks) unsalted butter, slightly softened

1 tbsp light brown sugar

¼ tsp pure vanilla extract

squeeze lemon juice

1oz (30g) pecans, toasted and roughly chopped

3oz (75g) dates, chopped into small pieces

to cook and serve:

flavorless oil or unsalted butter

maple syrup

1 To make the date and pecan butter, beat the butter until soft and slightly fluffy, then add the sugar, vanilla, and lemon juice. Stir in the pecans and dates. Cover and keep in the fridge (let it come to room temperature before you use it).

2 For the pancakes, sift the flour, baking powder, and salt into a bowl and mix in the sugar. Combine the rest of the ingredients together in a bowl, keeping the 2 egg whites separate. Make a well in the center of the bowl and gradually pour in the liquid, adding the dry ingredients to the well and gently whisking as you do so.

3 Beat the egg whites until they form soft peaks. Add 1 tbsp of the beaten whites to the batter to loosen it, then fold in the rest.

4 Heat a very small amount of butter or oil in a frying pan. Use about 4 tbsp batter per 3-inch (7.5-cm) pancake. Add as many pancakes as the pan will hold at one time. Cook for 2–3 minutes, until bubbles have appeared all over the surface and the pancakes have set underneath and are golden. Using a spatula flip each one over and cook on the other side until it is golden—about another minute. Add more butter or oil as needed.

5 As you cook the pancakes, top each one with a good dollop of pecan and date butter, stack them on top of each other, and keep warm in a low oven.

6 Serve with maple syrup drizzled over the whole stack and the rest of the butter on the side.

The cranberries look beautifully jewel-like on this cake. The fruit combination also works well in a tarte tatin.

PECAN AND PEAR UPSIDE-DOWN CAKE
with cranberries

serves 10

⅓ cup (5⅓ tbsp) butter

½ cup superfine sugar

2lb (900g) pears (about 6)

5oz (140g) cranberries

3oz (75g) shelled pecans

for the cake:

½ cup (1 stick) butter

1 cup superfine sugar

2 large eggs, separated

drop of vanilla extract

2 cups all-purpose flour

2 tsp baking powder

¾ cup milk

I Preheat the oven to 350°F (180°C). Melt the butter and sugar in a heavy-bottomed frying pan, about 10–12 inches (25–30cm) in diameter, over a low heat. Peel and core the pears and cut them into slices, about ½ inch (1cm) thick, and place them on top of the butter and sugar. Cook these over a gentle heat until just tender, then turn the heat up and cook them until lightly caramelized. Scatter the cranberries and pecans on top and gently mix all the fruit around.

2 For the cake, cream the butter and sugar and add the egg yolks in a mixer and a drop of vanilla. Mix in half the flour along with the baking powder. Add the milk and then the other half of the flour. Mix until smooth.

3 Beat the egg whites until they form medium peaks and, working quickly, fold into the cake mix with a large spoon.

4 Spread the batter over the pears and bake in the preheated oven for 35–40 minutes, or until a skewer inserted into the cake comes out clean.

5 Leave the cake to cool for 10 minutes before turning it out—but no longer, or the caramelized fruit will stick to the pan. If this does happen, carefully lever the pears off the pan and lay them on to the cake with their dark, caramelized side upwards.

I love the Italian Christmas sweetmeat, *panforte*, and wanted to make something more dessertlike with the same flavors. Serve this in small slices with whipped cream. If it's for adults, you could add a dash of booze—Amaretto or brandy—to the cake or to an accompanying cream.

ITALIAN CHRISTMAS CHOCOLATE CAKE
with chestnuts, hazelnuts, and walnuts

makes 1 cake

¾ cup (1½ sticks) unsalted butter

¾ cup superfine sugar

11½oz (325g) dark or semi-sweet chocolate, broken into pieces

2oz (50g) shelled walnuts, halved

2oz (50g) blanched almonds

75g (3oz) shelled hazelnuts

5 large eggs, separated

5½oz (150g) cooked chestnuts, broken into chunks

grated rind of 1 large orange

½ tsp ground cinnamon

2oz (50g) ground almonds

confectioners sugar for dusting or good-quality cooking chocolate, plus a few shelled hazelnuts and walnuts for decoration

1 Melt the butter and sugar in a bowl set over simmering water, then add the chocolate and melt it in the warm butter and sugar mixture, stirring to help it dissolve. Take it off the heat and let it cool slightly.

2 Preheat the oven to 350°F (180°C). Toast the nuts, except the chestnuts, in a dry pan, being careful that they don't burn. Break the nuts up very roughly—you want a mixture of large and smaller chunks, not chopped nuts.

3 Add the egg yolks to the chocolate mixture with the toasted nuts, chestnuts, orange rind, and cinnamon. Whisk the egg whites until stiff but not dry. Loosen the chocolate mixture by folding in 1 large spoonful of egg white, then fold in the rest, along with the ground almonds. Mix lightly so that you don't knock out the air. Pour into a buttered 8-inch (20-cm) springform cake pan and bake in the preheated oven for 45 minutes.

4 Leave the cake in the cake pan to cool for 20 minutes, then unclasp the spring-surround and remove the cake from the base. This is quite a fragile cake, with a mousselike middle, so handle it carefully.

5 The top will deflate and crack a little as the cake cools, but that's fine. Dust with confectioners sugar. Alternatively, if you want a glossy finish, melt some chocolate in a bowl set over a pan of simmering water. Spread the melted chocolate on to the cake and let it set. Roughly chop some hazelnuts and walnuts and scatter over the top.

"*First night of autumn*
the moon and pumpkins
face to face"
LEQUITA VANCE-WATKINS

EARTHLY PLEASURES
pumpkin, winter squash, beans, and lentils

Pumpkins and winter squash seem like a perfect metaphor for fall and winter cooking. The cook has the job of getting through that tough skin before finding the tender flesh, and they give of their best only after slow cooking. But it's worth it. They are great culinary chameleons, able to soak up and blend well with flavors as diverse as Gruyère, rosemary, sage, and nutmeg, and their smoky, nutty, sweet flavors perfectly match the autumnal months of mist and turning leaves. Their only limit is the cook's imagination. Confusion reigns, however, about the difference between a pumpkin and a winter squash. It is a difficult area, and often local usage dictates what is a squash and what is a pumpkin. Both are members of the same family, and although the terms are often used interchangeably, pumpkins are usually the jack-o'-lantern shape we associate with Halloween, while squashes can be smooth, warty, striped, stippled, their skins as green and shiny as old leather books, pale yellow, flame orange, or delicate amber. They come in myriad shapes—acorns, turbans, melons, and curled, snakelike creatures—and sizes. Each year, I display them before I cook them: a row is lined up on the wooden table in the hall; a great big *Rouge vif d'étampes*, the French variety that looks like Cinderella's carriage, acts as a doorstop between kitchen and living room; little miniature ones with cute names such as Munchkin, Jack-be-Little, and Baby Boo sit among the candles on the mantelpiece. Their flesh, once cooked, can be as smooth as that of avocado or baked quinces. The flavor may be sweet, nutty, cornlike, or, admittedly, bland, if you end up with a bad specimen.

The important matter for the cook is to find the varieties that he or she likes, be it a pumpkin or a winter squash. The best all-around variety, to my mind, is the Crown Prince. It's an elegant gray-blue, the sort of color you might find on a chart of historical paints, with not a hint of the vivid golden flesh inside. The ubiquitous butternut squash always has a great sweet taste and melting flesh, while the chubby, yellow-and-green striped Sweet Dumpling, and the marrowlike Delicata, are both excellent for stuffing and baking. You can get an even greater range from farmer's markets and specialist growers.

Leave the skin on winter squash and roast great smiling wedges of it with knobs of butter and maybe a light sprinkling of brown sugar or a drizzle of maple syrup, basting it every so often with the melted butter as they cook. Sauté chunks in butter or olive oil and sprinkle with garlic and parsley, or serve with pasta, cheese, and sage, or bake slices smothered in cream, Gruyère, and breadcrumbs.

You can also take full advantage of the shape of pumpkins and squashes as natural containers. Cut the top off little ones and, once you've scooped out the seeds and fibers, fill them with whipping cream and Gruyère or Parmesan, sautéed wild mushrooms, a part-cooked stuffing of wild and brown rice, dried cranberries and smoked bacon, or chopped spinach and ricotta. Replace the lids, roast under foil to stop the caramelized juices from burning, and serve as starters, or side dishes with pork or roast chicken. Even if I am going to purée the flesh, I either roast wedges or sauté chunks in butter rather than boiling. You need to drive off about a third of their moisture to intensify their taste, and anyway, that flesh loves butter, olive oil, and cream—you're never going to eat a low-cal pumpkin dish.

The Italians cook pumpkin and winter squash in risotto or mash the flesh, sweeten it with crushed *amaretti,* and use it to stuff pasta; the Belgians cook a *carbonnade* of beef and beer in a hollowed-out pumpkin; in southwest France they roast wedges in goose fat and thyme. In America, the homeland of pumpkin and winter squash, as well as sweet pumpkin pie there are savory pumpkin tarts, which are a great combination of salty and sweet, especially the ones made with strong cheese.

Then there is pumpkin soup. Using a base recipe of chopped pumpkin or winter squash sweated in butter with chopped leek and simmered in chicken stock. I turn out endless variations: try it with a dash of bourbon and a scattering of smoked bacon; serve one bubbling under a melting Gruyère crust or one topped with fried sage, Parmesan, and a drizzle of browned butter.

Nothing quite provides as much culinary succour as beans. I will never forget the first time I made *cassoulet,* the classic dish of southwest France. Rhythmically layering the parboiled beans with big handfuls of parsley and thyme, chunky sausages, sweet breast of lamb, and salty duck confit was soothing and earthing. Periodically stirring the pot to distribute the breadcrumb crust that forms on the top and acts as a thickener for the dish, I saw those firm white beans turn into the most unctuous food imaginable.

It's a pity we don't cook beans more often. Perhaps the soaking time puts us off: around 8 hours, though "overnight" seems to be the rule of thumb. You need to think ahead to have your soaked beans ready for a dish, though the quick-soak method means you can enjoy beans on the same day that you get the urge to eat them. Bring your beans up to the boil, take them off the heat, and leave them to soak for 2 hours.

Beans take time to cook, too, but you are rewarded with a soft, melting mass that has absorbed any flavor with which they were cooked—pork and lamb, olive oil, duck fat, garlic, tomatoes, onions, and herbs. In France, as well as the southwest's *cassoulet*-style dishes based on beans cooked with pork or duck, the Bretons and Normans pair navy and flageolet kidney beans with lamb. You would think eastern Europeans lived on bean soups, looking at how many there are in their repertoire. Beans also appear in side dishes there, especially with cabbage, and there's the Hungarian-style *cassoulet,* called *solet.* Tuscans are supposed to be the bean eaters of Italy, but you find plenty of beans in the northeast as well, particularly in the smoked bacon and cabbage soup, *jota.* In New England, debate rages from Boston to Maine about how to cook baked beans, and what variety of beans to bake, and local historical societies hold beans-in-the-hole bakes where beans are cooked in underground pits for 24 hours, just as in they were in the past.

Navy beans, which are also known as haricot or pea beans, are probably the most popular of all dried beans. They are small and white, not too starchy, and are used for baked beans and *cassoulet* (if you're in France, try to get the slightly larger *soisson* haricots). Cannellini beans are very similar to navy beans, but a little bit bigger, with a fluffier texture, and the flageolet, which is not the semi-dried version of the navy bean as some people think, but a distinct variety, is pale green with a creamy texture and a delicate flavor. Borlotti beans, which are also known as cranberry beans or roman beans, are large, pink speckled, and have a hammy, sweetly nutty flavor.

Lima beans, my least favorite, are big starchy beans with a thick skin and a potato-y flavor and are also called butter beans. They disintegrate easily, so do be careful when cooking them, but they're good with strong flavors such as mustard and chorizo. Their texture means that they can't really be used as a substitute for other white beans, however. Red kidney beans are mealy, with a distinctive meaty flavor, and they are used a lot in Georgian cooking to make salads for their *zakuski* (little mezze-style dishes), such as beans in sour plum sauce.

There are a few key things to watch out for when dealing with dried beans. Try to make sure they're not more than 6 months old; older than that and they take longer to cook, and some very old ones will never soften. Cook them in just enough water to cover them, but don't drown them, and cook them slowly. The best method is in a covered pan in a low oven—they seem to break up less and become more creamy—but slowly on the stove is okay. Keep checking them toward the end of the cooking time as age, length of soaking time, and variety all affect the length of time they need to cook. A bit of salt pork, pork fat, or olive oil, onion slices, spices, and herbs all give vital flavoring, and the beans need to be seasoned well about 15 minutes before the end of the cooking time. Not everyone agrees, but I am of the school that thinks that salt added to beans before they are cooked toughens them.

Lentils don't need soaking, so you can have a mound of nutty, smoky protein on your plate in 15 minutes, depending on the type of lentil you use. The orange ones become a lovely purée in that time and are delicious cooked in a little bit of stock, with perhaps the addition of a few cubes of smoked bacon, and make a superb soup made with ham stock, the shredded ham being stirred through just before serving.

There are also the large green or brown lentils, which are whole and unskinned and therefore retain their shape, though I usually hang the expense and go for Puy (also called French Green) or Umbrian lentils, the small, green-gray ones, the "*grand crus*" of the lentil world. They're fantastic with sausages, accompanied by Italian *mostarda* or sweet-and-sour figs, and with pot-roast guinea fowl, monkfish, or smoked haddock. I usually cook them with sautéed onion, carrot, celery, and pancetta in light chicken stock, though they also take well to being cooked in wine, or having mustard and cream added at the end. Cooked quite plainly and then doused in vinaigrette (dress lentils while still warm so they absorb the flavors), they make wonderful salads.

Lentils have become increasingly hip—especially the fancier ones—but bean esteem is low. It shouldn't be. The reaction you get from family and friends as you lift the lid off a dish of *cassoulet* or a pot of Vermont maple baked beans on a cold winter's day is an indication of how much we yearn for them. They may not make for instant eating, but there is something almost primeval in our desire for such culinary comfort.

Warm winter squash is a surprisingly successful salad ingredient. The big golden wedges look beautiful and make a good partner for all kinds of salty, earthy ingredients. Try it in salads with nuts and strong cheeses, wild mushrooms, baby spinach, and smoked chicken or duck.

You can replace the goat cheese here with a blue cheese if you prefer. Use a winter squash with a good, sweet flavor, such as butternut or Crown Prince.

ROAST WINTER SQUASH SALAD
with lentils and goat cheese

serves 6

3lb 5oz (1.5kg) winter squash, such as butternut or acorn

salt and pepper

olive oil

2 tbsp butter

9oz (250g) goat cheese, broken into small nuggets

for the lentils:

9¾oz (275g) green lentils, Puy or Umbrian

½ small onion, very finely chopped

1 small celery stalk, very finely chopped

1 tbsp butter

½ tbsp olive oil

1½ tbsp finely chopped fresh flat-leaf parsley

for the dressing:

½ tbsp white wine vinegar

tiny dollop Dijon mustard

4 tbsp extra virgin olive oil

good pinch superfine sugar

I Preheat the oven to 350°F (180°C). Halve the winter squash and scoop out the seeds and fibers. Cut each half into 1-inch (2.5-cm) wedges and then peel each one. You should have about 2lb (900g) of prepared flesh.

2 Put the squash wedges in a roasting tray, season, drizzle with olive oil, and dot with butter. Roast in the preheated oven for 15–20 minutes, turning the wedges over in the fat from time to time until the squash is just tender. Don't let it scorch or get too dry.

3 Prepare the lentils while the squash is cooking. Rinse, then cover them with cold water, bring to the boil, and cook until tender, which can take anything from 15–30 minutes. The lentils should hold their shape, so keep checking them. While the lentils are cooking, gently sauté the onion and celery in the butter and oil until they are soft but not colored.

4 Make the dressing by whisking all the ingredients together. Season.

5 When the lentils are cooked, add them to the pan of onion and celery and stir them around to soak up the cooking juices. Add two-thirds of the dressing and the chopped parsley and season really well with salt and pepper.

6 Put a small mound of lentils on each plate and top with the roast pumpkin, cut into cubes if you prefer. Dot with the nuggets of goat cheese, drizzle each plate with the remaining dressing and serve.

We grow a lot of pumpkin and winter squash, so pumpkin soup is always on the go in our house in the fall. Which recipe to give you was a headache. Should it be Italian-style with fried sage, brown butter, and Parmesan, a French one under a molten crust of Gruyère, or one with the American flavors of maple-cured bacon and bourbon? In the end, this version from Normandy won the day. It tastes great and looks stunning.

PUMPKIN SOUP
with mussels

serves 6

½ cup (1 stick) butter

2 leeks, washed, trimmed, and sliced into rounds

1 onion, roughly chopped

2lb 4oz (1kg) pumpkin or winter squash flesh, cut into chunks (from approx. 3lb 5oz/1.5kg pumpkin or squash)

3lb 5oz (1.5kg) mussels

½ onion, finely chopped

1 celery stalk, finely chopped

2 garlic cloves, sliced

handful parsley stalks

1 cup dry white wine

freshly ground black pepper

½ cup heavy cream

6 tbsp chopped flat-leaf parsley

good squeeze lemon

to serve

heavy cream

I Melt 3 tbsp butter in a heavy saucepan and add the leeks and half the onion. Cover and sweat over a low heat for 12 minutes, adding a splash of water every so often to stop the mixture from catching.

2 Add another 3 tbsp butter and allow it to melt, then add the squash. Cover and sweat for 15 minutes, again adding splashes of water and stirring from time to time.

3 Wash the mussels, remove any beards, and discard any that are damaged or that do not close when tapped against the side of the sink. Melt the rest of the butter in a large pan and add the rest of the onion, the celery, garlic, and parsley stalks. Stir over a low heat until softened, then add the mussels and wine. Cover and cook over a medium heat for 4 minutes, until they have opened.

4 Drain the mussels, collecting the liquor, and strain the liquor through a sieve lined with muslin. Taste the liquor; if it's very salty, don't use it all. Make the liquid up to 4¾ cups by adding water.

5 Add the mussel stock to the pan with the squash and bring the soup to the boil. Add pepper (you're unlikely to need salt), simmer until the pumpkin or squash flesh is soft, then let the soup cool and purée in a blender. Add the cream and check the seasoning.

6 Take most of the mussels out of their shells, discarding any that have not opened and keep a few in their shells—it just looks good. Add the mussels to the soup and gently heat through, stirring in the parsley. If the soup is too thick, add enough water to bring it to a consistency you like. Add a good squeeze of lemon, check the seasoning, and serve with a swirl of cream in each bowl.

Matefaims—they can be translated as "hunger-killers", from the French "*mater la faim*"—are thick pancakes from the Savoie region of France, made with potatoes, cornmeal, buckwheat, or root vegetables. They're used in an elegant way in this dish, but you can also make real mountain dishes from them: try *matefaims* with thick slices of cooked ham and melting cheese, for example; great after a day on the slopes.

JUNIPER-ROAST QUAIL
with pumpkin *matefaims*

serves 6

12 quails

½ cup brandy

leaves from 3 sprigs fresh thyme

salt and pepper

¼ cup (½ stick) butter

1 small onion, very finely chopped

3½oz (100g) good-quality cooked or cured ham, such as Parma ham

10 juniper berries, crushed

1 cup dry white wine

1½ cups heavy cream

2 tbsp finely chopped flat-leaf parsley, for serving

for the *matefaims*:

¾ cup all-purpose flour

¾ cup buttermilk

salt and pepper

2 eggs and 1 extra egg white

9oz (250g) cooked, mashed pumpkin

generous grating fresh nutmeg

¼ cup (½ stick) unsalted butter, softened

1 Rub the quails, inside and out, with the brandy and thyme and season. Leave to marinate, loosely covered, in the fridge, overnight.

2 Preheat the oven to 350°F (180°C). Melt the butter in a casserole in which all the quails fit snugly and brown the birds on all sides. Set the birds aside and cook the onion in the same pan until soft and just beginning to turn golden. Cut the ham into fine shreds and add it to the pot with the juniper berries. Pour in the wine and bring to simmering point. Put the quails in the pot, cover, and cook in the oven for 30 minutes, until the juices between the thigh and the body are clear.

3 To make the *matefaims*, simply mix together all the ingredients except the extra egg white until well combined and smooth. When you are nearly ready to serve the pancakes, beat the egg white until you have soft peaks and fold into the mixture. You can leave the mixture like this, covered, while the birds are cooking.

4 Remove the birds from the pot and keep them, covered, in a low oven while you quickly make the sauce. Just add the cream to the pot and simmer, stirring, until it has thickened slightly. Add the quails back to the pot, cover, and keep warm.

5 Heat a good pat of the butter in a frying pan and add small ladlefuls of batter to make pancakes about 4 inches (10cm) in diameter. Cook a couple of pancakes at a time until golden and set on one side, then flip the pancakes over and cook on the other side. Add butter when you need it and be careful not to let it burn.

6 Serve 1 or 2 pancakes per person with 2 quails on top and some sauce spooned over. Scatter the parsley on top.

Pumpkins and winter squash are great in tarts. It's that mixture of the sweet and the salty in savory pumpkin pies that really gets me. This makes one large pie or six small ones.

PUMPKIN TARTS
with spinach and Gorgonzola

serves 6

for the pastry:

2 cups all-purpose flour

¾ cup (1½ sticks) butter

good pinch salt

a little very cold water

for the filling:

1lb (450g) pumpkin or winter squash, such as butternut

olive oil

450g (1lb) spinach

2 large eggs plus 1 egg yolk

1¼ cups heavy cream

2oz (50g) Parmesan, grated

freshly grated nutmeg

7oz (200g) Gorgonzola

I For the pastry, put the flour, butter, and salt into the food processor and, using the plastic blade, process the mixture until it resembles breadcrumbs. Add just enough water to make the pastry come together. Wrap it in tin foil or plastic wrap and refrigerate for about half an hour.

2 Preheat the oven to 350°F (180°C). Cut your pumpkin from top to bottom into broad slices, remove the inner stringy bits and seeds, and peel. Brush lightly with olive oil and bake in the preheated oven for 20 minutes, or until just tender. Destalk and wash the spinach. Put it into a large saucepan, cover, and wilt in the water left clinging to it (about 4 minutes over a medium heat). Drain well and leave to cool.

3 Make the custard by mixing together the whole eggs, egg yolk, cream, and Parmesan. Season well. Roll out the rested pastry and line a tart pan 9 inches (23cm) in diameter and 1½ inches (4cm) deep. Chill for another 30 minutes (or just stick it in the freezer for about 15 minutes). Prick the bottom of the tart and bake blind—line the pastry with greaseproof paper and put ceramic baking beans or ordinary dried beans on top—in the preheated oven for 7 minutes. Remove the paper and beans and cook for another 4 minutes.

4 Cut the pumpkin into small slices, about 4 inches (10cm) long and ½ inch (1cm) thick. Squeeze every last bit of water from the spinach and chop it up. Season both of these and add some freshly grated nutmeg to the spinach. Spread the spinach over the bottom of the tart case, then add the slices of pumpkin and dot with nuggets of Gorgonzola. Pour the custard mixture over the tart and bake, again at 350°F (180°C), for 40 minutes for 1 large pie and 25–30 minutes for smaller ones, or until the pastry is golden. Leave for 10 minutes to let the custard finish cooking and set a little once you have taken it out of the oven.

Swedes go misty-eyed when they talk about this soup. For years it was the traditional Thursday night meal, usually followed by Swedish pancakes, and it still is in many homes. You can either cook a ham shank for both the stock and the meat to go into the soup, or you can get a ham bone for the stock—even the bone from a Parma ham—and buy separate ham, pork, or bacon to put into it.

SWEDISH THURSDAY SOUP
with split peas and ham

serves 6–8

2 tbsp butter

1 onion, finely chopped

2 leeks, washed and roughly chopped

3 garlic cloves, finely chopped

5 cups stock, preferably made using a ham bone

10oz (280g) split peas, soaked overnight, drained and rinsed

8oz (225g) each of carrot and celeriac, cut into dice

5½oz (150g) cooked smoked ham or pork, shredded, or ½-inch (1-cm) cubes of smoked bacon

1 Melt the butter in a heavy-bottomed pan, add the onion, leeks, and a splash of water and sweat the vegetables, covered, over a low heat until sweet and soft (about 15 minutes). Check from time to time to make sure the onions have enough moisture in them to prevent them from burning. Add another splash of water if you need to. Add the garlic and sauté in the buttery juices for a couple of minutes, then add the stock and the split peas.

2 Cook the soup for an hour, then add the diced carrot and celeriac and cook for another 30 minutes. The vegetables should be soft and the split peas disintegrating.

3 If you've made the stock with a ham shank, then add some of the ham from that bone. Otherwise add the cooked pork and heat that through, or sauté bacon in its own fat until browned on all sides then add that to the soup.

4 This soup can be served with sour cream, but I prefer it properly hearty and unadorned.

"Hunger makes beans taste like almonds"

ITALIAN FOLK SAYING

Look at the ingredients list for this recipe and you might think: "Beans, bacon, and lettuce that go soggy in hot stock—big deal!". And it's from a country not known for its cuisine. But it is one of my favorite dishes in this book. It presents a combination of flavors that we just aren't used to—pork, beans, vinegar, sour cream, and dill—and is rich and warming. You'll love it.

ROMANIAN BEAN, SMOKED BACON,
and sour cream soup

serves 6–8

2 tbsp butter

1 onion, finely chopped

2 celery stalks, finely chopped

7oz (200g) smoked pancetta or bacon, rind removed and cut into large cubes

8oz (225g) dried navy beans, soaked overnight

6 cups chicken stock

salt and pepper

1 little gem lettuce, or ½ romaine lettuce

¾ cup sour cream

1 tbsp white wine vinegar

small bunch fresh dill, chopped

1 Melt the butter in a heavy-bottomed pan and add the onion and celery. Turn the vegetables over in the butter, add a splash of water, and cover the pan. Cook the vegetables over a very low heat until sweet and soft—about 15 minutes. Check from time to time to make sure the onion has enough moisture in it to prevent it from burning. Add another splash of water if you need to.

2 Sauté the pancetta or bacon in its own fat in another pan until it is colored all over. Add to the vegetables once they have sweated enough.

3 Drain the beans of their soaking water and add them to the pan. Cover with the stock, bring to the boil, and then turn down to a simmer. Cook, partially covered, for 1½–2 hours, or until the beans are soft. Mash them up a little with a potato masher just to break them down. Season well with salt and pepper.

4 Shred the lettuce and add it to the soup along with the sour cream and the vinegar. Reheat gently, add the dill, and serve.

I often feel like eating *cassoulet* but can't be bothered to make it, so I was thrilled to eat *sobronade* the last time I was in southwest France. It's a kind of everyday *cassoulet* (without the goose or duck *confit*) that nevertheless has the same satisfying warmth. Perfect for Halloween.

Use a mixture of butter and oil, or rendered pork fat, if you don't have goose or duck fat, but you can buy duck and goose fat in cans. Freeze whatever fat you don't need for future use.

SOBRONADE

serves 8

2 onions

3 large carrots

1lb 2oz (500g) celeriac

10½oz (300g) rutabaga

10½oz (300g) waxy potatoes

¼ cup goose or duck fat

500g (1lb 2oz) pork belly, skinned, boned and cut into chunks

9oz (250g) navy beans, soaked overnight

4 garlic cloves, finely sliced

small bunch fresh flat-leaf parsley

leaves from 6 sprigs thyme

2 bay leaves

1lb 12oz (800g) hot pork sausages

1 x 16-oz can tomatoes in thick juice

1 Peel and cut 1 onion into quarters; roughly chop the other. Peel and cut the carrots, celeriac, and rutabaga into roughly ¾ inch (2cm) cubes. Cut the potatoes into chunks.

2 Melt 1 tbsp of the goose or duck fat in a very large, heavy-bottomed casserole and lightly brown the pork belly all over. Drain and rinse the beans and add to the pork. Add the quartered onion and cover with water, up to about 1 inch (2.5cm) above the level of the beans. Bring slowly to the boil, skim well, and turn down to a simmer.

3 Meanwhile, melt 2 tbsp of the goose or duck fat in a frying pan and lightly brown the chopped onion, carrots, celeriac, and rotabaga in batches, adding the vegetables to the pork and bean pot as they are ready. Add half of the sliced garlic, the finely chopped stalks of parsley, the thyme, and the bay leaves. Stir, cover, and simmer for 1 hour, stirring occasionally.

4 Brown the sausages in a hot pan in the rest of the goose or duck fat. Slice into chunks and add to the pot along with the tomatoes, the potatoes, and the rest of the parsley, roughly chopped. Stir and season really well with salt and pepper (beans need a lot of seasoning). Leave the lid off so that the liquid can reduce and simmer for a further half hour, stirring from time to time. Check the seasoning and serve.

New Englanders are every bit as deserving of the title "bean eaters" as Tuscans. According to the American food writer, John Thorne, how you cook your beans is a major topic of conversation in small-town Maine. Though Boston baked beans are famous, most rural New Englanders are derisory about them, feeling that you are more likely to find canned beans in the city than good home-baked beans. Bean cookers have strong opinions about which variety of bean—Jacob's cattle beans, soldier beans, Vermont cranberry beans, yellow-eye beans, and so on—works best, and maple syrup and cider jelly are used just as often as molasses in the various versions.

Pork and beans baked in a bean hole, a stone-lined pit filled with logs burned down to charcoal, was such a popular dish for loggers and lumberjacks to cook while working that it was sometimes eaten three times a day, so you could say New Englanders have beans in their soul.

VERMONT BAKED BEANS

serves 6

1lb 2oz (500g) navy beans, soaked overnight

1lb 2oz (500g) salt pork or unsmoked bacon in the piece

4 garlic cloves, finely chopped

3 cups tomato purée

3 tbsp maple syrup

3 tbsp molasses

3 tbsp dry English mustard

3 tbsp cider vinegar

2 bay leaves

salt and pepper

6 cloves

2 onions, quartered

3 tbsp roughly chopped fresh flat-leaf parsley

1 Drain and rinse the beans and put them in a large, heavy-bottomed casserole dish. Add enough water to cover them by about 2 inches (5cm) and bring to the boil. Boil hard for 10 minutes, then turn the heat down to a simmer, cover and cook for about an hour, or until the beans are tender but not completely soft. Check the water to ensure the beans don't boil dry.

2 Preheat the oven to 275°F (140°C).

3 Cut the pork or bacon into 2 inch (5cm) cubes and add it to the beans along with the garlic, tomato purée, maple syrup, molasses, mustard, vinegar, bay leaves, and pepper (don't add salt yet as you need to see how salty the beans become being cooked with the salt pork or bacon). Stick the cloves into the quartered onions and add them too. Add more water if you need to, so that the beans are covered. Replace the lid, put the casserole dish in the preheated oven, and bake for 2 hours. Remove the lid, stir, and put the casserole dish back in the oven for another hour to brown and thicken. Check during this last hour to make sure the beans aren't becoming too dry. Taste for seasoning and stir in the parsley.

"Now the potatoes and carrots, the beets and turnips and cabbages were gathered and stored in the cellar, for freezing nights had come."

LITTLE HOUSE IN THE BIG WOODS LAURA INGALLS WILDER

FIELD DAYS
winter vegetables

My earliest memories are of running in and out of our back garden, misty and smoky with the smell of coal fires, while my mother put clothes on the washing line and chastised me for not eating my carrots. "You see those big crows up there?" she'd ask. They were lined up, black-caped and evil-looking, cawing on the telephone wires. "Well, they carry little girls away if they don't eat their carrots." I had visions of being picked up by the shoulders of my cardigan and hoisted aloft, clinging to the plate of carrots that had wrought my demise.

It's amazing that I like carrots at all, given my crow experiences, but they're one of my favorite vegetables. I'd rather eat roast chicken with mashed potato and buttery carrots than almost anything else. I most often prepare them as they were at the spas at Vichy in France, mixed with butter, sugar, and a little water, which evaporates during cooking. This method induces even my six-year-old to declare that he couldn't live without them.

Why do we despise winter vegetables—roots in particular? Maybe it's that unfortunate little quirk of human nature that makes us undervalue what is beneath our noses. Certainly our cold-weather vegetables provide more interesting and fitting dishes than the exotic interlopers that are flown halfway around the world to "brighten" the darker months. Look at the colours for a start: the vivid orange of carrots, the magenta of beets, the mauve-tinged greenness of curly-leaved cabbages. I get as much pleasure out of dealing with these as I do from spring and summer vegetables. Of course we love such vegetables as asparagus, peas, and broad beans. The season and our bodies compel us toward them; but we also appreciate them because their appearance is fleeting. If potatoes, with their soft, milky-tasting flesh, were only available for six weeks in the year, we'd be crazy about them, too.

Root vegetables bring sweet sustenance to a cold, gray world. Roasted, the sugars in them become so concentrated and caramelized that you have to push them with a spoon to dislodge their sticky bodies from the pan. They are easily as good as a plateful of roasted Mediterranean vegetables. And roasting is just the beginning. Carrots are good cooked with a splash of orange juice and a drizzle of honey or simmered in stock and mixed with wild mushrooms and cream to make *carottes à la forestière*. A classic candidate for roasting is the parsnip, a vegetable which American and British diners seem to be alone in liking. They can be roasted with brown sugar or maple syrup, or boiled, mashed with butter and cinnamon, and crowned with a pile of sweet, browned onions. It is funny that the Russians have never really gone for the parsnip, given that the Russian word for them is *pasternak*. You'd think that a vegetable with the same name as the author of the romantic *Dr. Zhivago* would have a better image, but apparently not.

Americans and Brits are supposed to love our potatoes, but we see them largely as mopper-uppers of other flavors; the support act rather than the star. It's a pity when you think of what can be done with them. The Savoie and *Dauphiné* regions of France have bubbling potato gratins; in the southwest of France they sauté them to an awesome richness in goose fat; in Italy they make gnocchi and croquettes from potatoes; and Russians fry them with wild mushrooms. The Scandinavians, like Americans amd Brits, eat them at practically every meal, baking slices in dill-flavored béchamel sauce to serve with pork, for example. The Swiss and the Dutch cook them with pears and apples for just the same purpose. In Hungary and Austria, potatoes are sautéed with paprika or caraway seeds, bathed in warm sour cream with nuggets of pickled cucumber, and mashed with curd cheese and chunks of Speck. There's so much more to potatoes than mashed and roasted.

Then there are the more *recherché* roots. Jerusalem artichokes, looking like knobbly potatoes wearing coats lent to them by root ginger, are more nuttily sweet than any other vegetable and have melting, ivory-colored flesh. They're good paired with salty or meaty ingredients: try them sliced and sautéed with bacon or mushrooms, or use them to replace some of the potatoes in a *gratin dauphinoise*, or to make a lovely tawny soup. They're the devil to peel, though—so I often don't. Flecks of beige in a soup or purée won't hurt anyone, and roasted whole with little branches of thyme, the skin of a Jerusalem artichoke is as good as the flesh. Celeriac, a form of celery bred specially for its bulbous base, is also underused. Its celery flavor can be almost overwhelming and it needs strong foods such as game to stand up to it, but it's great tempered with potato and produces a mash with a real herby edge.

At one time I saw beets just as a salad ingredient pickled to within an inch of its life. Then I went to Scandinavia. One of the first meals I enjoyed in Sweden was a simple plate of hot-smoked trout, potatoes dressed with dill and sour cream, and some globes of roasted beets, warm, crimson, and still in their skins. What a partner they were for the salty smokiness of the fish, the aniseedy freshness of dill, and the cold starkness of sour cream! I've also, in Denmark, had chopped beetroot mixed with capers to accompany cod with mustard sauce and, in Austria, eaten hot-roast beets dressed with seasoned buttermilk alongside roast pork. Russians and Poles love beets, too, using it in their famous *borscht* and as a partner for game, and Georgians grate and purée it to make salads and dips for their little mezze-style dishes, *zakuski*. If you don't cook beets, then give them a try: the color is magnificent and their charms don't stop there.

It's a family joke that every time my father sits down to turnips, he comments (always as if for the first time): "It's a very underrated vegetable, turnip." We all snicker, but I have to concur. Parboiled and fried with chunks of bacon, a good pat of butter and a shower of black pepper, it's surely worthy of more than feeding to pigs. Rutagaba is even better—it is sweeter—though both do have a slight peppery bitterness that is perhaps an acquired taste.

The old-fashioned preparation of cabbage—the smell, the lack of seasoning, the bitter taste of the waterlogged slop that ends up on your plate—should put everyone off this vegetable for life. But there are so many excellent eastern European cabbage dishes that, even if you think you hate it, you must give it another try. Crinkly, squeaky Savoy, shredded and cooked briskly—and I mean for just 4 minutes—in a tablespoon of water, a good pat of butter and flavorings such as crushed juniper berries, is a world away from the wtered-down stuff. In Hungary, I've had Savoy sautéed with onions and caraway seeds; in Russia, baked with apples and sour cream; and in Norway, sweated in butter with bacon and dill. Red cabbage gets the classic fruit treatment in Great Britain and all over eastern Europe, but it's also good with bacon, caraway and a dollop of sour cream, or with cranberries, pears, or orange instead of the usual apple. And juniper loves it just as much as a Savoy.

Purple-sprouting broccoli, another member of the cabbage family, appears in March and, though some regard it as a spring vegetable, I feel it is firmly placed earlier, at the brighter end of winter. We grow loads of it in our garden and, while I never use it for anything complicated, I can't get enough. Its slender shape means that you can half-sauté and half-sweat it in olive oil and a splash of white wine: no full-scale steaming or boiling.

Despite the fact that *vichyssoise* is a summer soup, leeks are at their best from October to March and a pot of warm, creamy leek-and-potato soup is even better than its cold counterpart. This is a veg that, I'm afraid, is greatly enhanced by butter, and leeks do need to be softened in it to get the best out of them. Sweat shredded leeks in a covered pan with a splash of water and a good chunk of butter for a sloppy purée to serve with fish, or mix the softened veg with Savoy cabbage, drizzle with cream, and bake under slices of melting fontina or Taleggio cheese. Leeks are often a good extra ingredient, perfuming the rest of a dish with a mild onion flavor: try layering them with potatoes and cheese in a cream or stock-based gratin and you'll see what I mean. They make a great quiche-style tart too, especially if you spread a big spoonful of grain mustard into the pastry case before filling it.

Everywhere I went in snowy northern Italy I found radicchio, a vegetable I hadn't associated with cold weather. As well as the ubiquitous round *Radicchio di Chioggia* you're able to buy other varieties at good grocery stores: *Rosso di Verona*, with its spear-shaped leaves and slightly more delicate flavor; *Rosso di Castelfranco*, a round roselike variety; and *Rosso di Treviso*, which resembles a little bush with long, pointed leaves and broad ivory ribs. They all look spectacular, with their crimson-splattered creaminess. The Verona and Treviso varieties are great with nuts, pomegranates, and smoked food, and they find their way into winter salads. The various forms of radicchio are also sautéed or grilled and served as a side dish. This treatment softens their bitterness and turns their edges into brown, wilting leaves.

I also love the long, pale, bitter endive or chicory. Its flavor renders it truly wintry—that bite is like a cold gust of wind—and it's a great palate cleanser in a season when dishes are cooked to softness and sweetness. Left in chicons, it seems to last for ages in the bottom of the fridge and can be used in salads or braised in butter and bacon, maybe adding a little cream, or even orange juice for a side dish with attitude.

Frisée, that mad, tangled mess of a lettuce, is another perfect choice for fall and winter salads, especially those that contain apples, pears, or cheese with a bit of bite as its bitterness can take on strong flavors. My staple winter salad leaf, though, is watercress. Its dark green color, the sturdiness of its stems, its strong minerally taste, make it seem more appropriate for winter than summer eating. And on days when you want mouthfuls of healthy, uncooked greenery, you can serve it with hot roasts and grilled meats. The wilting leaves seem even better soaked in warm meaty cooking juices than a zippy vinaigrette.

Alternating with the Irish potato dish champ, this was the winter staple for Saturday lunch when I was growing up, and we still fight over it when we are all at home. Every Irish family has a different idea of how Irish stew should be done, and everyone thinks their version is right, so obviously this is the only recipe you should ever follow. Sweet and lamby and completely satisfying.

IRISH STEW

serves 6

3lb 4oz (1.4kg) lamb shanks or middle neck of lamb

handful parsley stalks

3 large onions, peeled

1lb 2oz (500g) carrots, peeled

6 black peppercorns

3 very large floury potatoes, peeled

salt and pepper

leaves from 3 sprigs fresh thyme

finely chopped fresh flat-leaf parsley, to serve

I Put the lamb in a large saucepan with the parsley stalks, 1 onion (halved), 1 large carrot (halved), and the peppercorns. Cover with water, bring to the boil and skim. Turn the heat down to a simmer, cover, and cook the lamb over a very gentle heat until it is completely tender and almost falling off the bone. It should take about 1–1¼ hours.

2 Remove the lamb from the stock and strain the stock. Cut the remaining carrots into small chunks, the potatoes into big chunks, and the remaining onions into half-moon shaped slices. Put these into a clean saucepan, add the stock, and season with salt and pepper. Cook until the vegetables are tender and the potatoes have partially fallen apart, stirring from time to time. You need them to fall apart a little in order to thicken the stew.

3 While the vegetables are cooking, remove all the lamb from the bones and cut it into large, irregular chunks. Add the meat to the stew along with the thyme leaves, salt, and pepper. Heat through and check the seasoning. Scatter with the parsley and serve.

"He said he would show us what could be done up the river in the way of cooking, and suggested that, with the vegetables and the remains of the cold beef and general odds and ends, we should make an Irish stew... The job turned out to be the biggest thing of its kind that I had ever been in. We began cheerfully, one might almost say skittishly, but our lightheartedness was gone by the time the first potato was finished. The more we peeled, the more peel there seemed to be left on; by the time we had got all the peel off and all the eyes out, there was no potato left..."

THREE MEN IN A BOAT JEROME K. JEROME

Knödel are dumplings, known elsewhere in Italy as gnocchi or *canderli*, from the Alto Adige. This recipe is from chef Alois Rottensteiner, who has a lovely farmhouse restaurant near Bolzano called Patscheider Hof. They serve both types of *knödel* together. If you can't get hold of Quark use two parts ricotta cheese mixed with one part sour cream.

TWO TYROLEAN KNÖDEL

spinach and cheese *knödel*

serves 6

½ tbsp olive oil

½ small onion, very finely chopped

1 garlic clove, minced

1lb 2oz (500g) spinach, destalked

9oz (250g) white breadcrumbs

4½oz (125g) Quark cheese

½ cup whole milk

2 eggs, beaten

⅓ cup all-purpose flour

good grating nutmeg

salt and pepper

melted butter and grated Parmesan, to serve

1 Heat the oil in a frying pan and sweat the onion very gently until soft but not colored. Add the garlic and cook for a further minute.

2 Cook the spinach in a covered saucepan with the water that is left clinging to the leaves after washing. It will take about 4 minutes to wilt on a medium heat. Turn the spinach over halfway through cooking. Leave to cool, then squeeze out as much water as possible. Chop finely.

2 Mix all the ingredients, except the butter and Parmesan, together in a bowl and season well.

3 With wet hands, form dumplings about the size of a walnut and place these on a floured baking tray. Bring a saucepan of salted water up to the boil, then turn the water down to a simmer. Poach the dumplings for about 5 minutes—they will float to the surface when they are ready. Serve with plenty of melted butter and grated Parmesan.

beet *knödel*

serves 6

½ tbsp olive oil

½ small onion, very finely chopped

1 garlic clove, minced

10½oz (300g) cooked and peeled beets (see page 76)

7oz (200g) white breadcrumbs

½ cup milk

1 egg, beaten

2 tbsp flour

melted butter and grated Parmesan, to serve

1 Heat the oil in a frying pan and sweat the onion very gently until soft but not colored. Add the garlic and cook for a further minute. Chop the beets into tiny cubes.

2 Mix all the ingredients, except the butter and Parmesan, together in a bowl and season well.

3 With wet hands, form dumplings about the size of a walnut and place these on a floured baking tray. Bring a saucepan of salted water up to the boil, then turn the water down to a simmer. Poach the dumplings for about 5 minutes—they will float to the surface when they are ready. Serve with plenty of melted butter and grated Parmesan.

Carrots cooked with butter, a little sugar, and liquid that evaporates during cooking is one of my favorite vegetable dishes. This recipe makes them just a little bit more special.

FARMER'S CARROTS with bacon and parsley

serves 4

12oz (350g) carrots, peeled

1½ cups chicken stock

4oz (115g) unsmoked bacon lardons

2 tbsp heavy cream

squeeze of lemon

1 tbsp finely chopped fresh flat-leaf parsley

pepper

1 Cut the carrots into batons. Put them in a heavy-bottomed saucepan, add the stock, and bring to the boil. Cook until the carrots are tender. You may need to add a little more water, but the idea is for all the cooking liquid to evaporate.

2 In a frying pan over medium heat, quickly sauté the bacon in its own fat until well colored all over. Add the bacon, cream, lemon, parsley, and pepper to the carrots (you shouldn't need salt because the stock is so reduced). Stir and let the cream bubble away a little until you just have a thick coating on the carrots. Serve immediately.

A great spin on regular olive oil roast potatoes and a cinch to make, this is good with any cut of pork and with roast chicken.

HUNGARIAN POTATOES
with paprika and caraway seeds

serves 4

14oz (400g) small waxy potatoes

2 onions, peeled

2 tsp caraway seeds, roughly crushed

1 tsp each, hot paprika and sweet paprika

salt and pepper

2 tbsp olive oil or rendered pork fat

1 Preheat the oven to 350°F (180°C). Cut any larger potatoes in half—you want all of them to be roughly the same size—and cut the onions in half-moon-shaped slices, about ⅔ inch (1.5cm) thick at the thickest part.

2 Mix everything together in a roasting tray. Put into the oven for about 25–30 minutes, or until the potatoes are cooked through and dark gold. Shake the tray and stir the potatoes around every so often. The onions will char a little at the tips, but that adds a good flavor. You can serve them daubed with a little sour cream.

For comfort in a pot, nothing beats mashed potatoes. Nothing sits more easily in your stomach or is less demanding to eat. This horseradish version is great with beef and the mustard one is good with pork and chicken. *Aligot*, a classic dish from southwest France, is traditionally eaten on its own, but it's also good with pork, and buttermilk mash is gloriously tangy and goes with anything. Irish champ is what we used to eat for Saturday lunch as soon as floury potatoes were in season. (we were always asking my mum whether it was "champ time" yet). It's awfully bad for you, but you must serve it in big mounds with a hollow in the middle in which you melt yet more butter, then dip each forkful into this golden pool before eating it. Use floury potatoes such as White Rose, Yukon Gold, or Red Rose.

ALL KINDS OF MASH

all serve 4–6

4½oz (125g) scallions, cut into rings

½ cup whole milk

2lb (900g) mashing potatoes

½ cup (1 stick) butter

salt and pepper

extra butter, for serving

champ

1 Put the green onions in a saucepan with the milk and heat on the stove until boiling. Take off the heat and leave the onions to infuse the milk for about 30 minutes.

2 Cook the potatoes in boiling, lightly salted water until tender, then drain and remove the skins. Put the potatoes back in the saucepan and cover them with a clean dish towel and a lid. Put them back on a very low heat for a couple of minutes to let the potatoes dry out a bit—this gives a better mash.

3 Mash the potatoes with the butter until no lumps are left. Heat the milk and green onions again, then gradually beat this into the potatoes, mixing well with a wooden spoon to make the potatoes fluffy. Season well. This is good with bacon or thick slices of ham and, though it's not traditional, I also like it with fish.

"I have friends who begin with pasta, and friends who begin with rice, but whenever I fall in love, I begin with potatoes. Sometimes meat and potatoes and sometimes fish and potatoes, but always potatoes. I have made a lot of mistakes falling in love, and regretted most of them, but never the potatoes that went with them."

HEARTBURN NORA EPHRON

½ cup heavy cream

¼ cup milk

2lb (900g) mashing potatoes

⅓ cup (5⅓ tbsp) butter

2 tbsp freshly grated
horseradish, ready-grated
horseradish from a jar, or
creamed horseradish

salt and pepper

horseradish mash

Make the mash in the same way as in the previous recipe, but this time heat the cream and milk together and add this to the mashed potatoes instead of the green onion and milk mixture. Stir in the horseradish after mashing in the butter and season with salt and pepper.

mustard mash

Make as above, beating in 3 tbsp wholegrain mustard instead of horseradish.

buttermilk mash

Make as for the horseradish mash, but omit the milk. Add the heated cream, then ½ cup cold buttermilk. Do not add horseradish.

aligot

Make as for the horseradish mash, stirring in 3 cloves of finely chopped garlic instead of horseradish. Then, over a low heat, add 15oz (425g) sliced *Tomme Fraîche* cheese from Cantal. Beat the mixture as if you were beating egg whites. Eventually, as the cheese melts and you incorporate air, the mixture will look sticky and shiny and will come away from the sides of the pan. It should have almost a pouring consistency. Check the seasoning and eat immediately.

3 large heads garlic

olive oil

salt and pepper

2lb 4oz (1kg) parsnips, peeled

2 tbsp butter

4 tbsp heavy cream

parsnip and roast garlic mash

1 Preheat the oven to 350°F (180°C). Put the heads of garlic into a small roasting tray, without removing any of their outer papery skin or separating any cloves. Generously drizzle with olive oil, season, and add about 4 tbsp water to the tray. Bake in the preheated oven for 40–50 minutes, or until the heads are completely soft. Keep checking the tray to make sure that there is still some liquid in it.

2 Chop the parsnips into large chunks, then either steam or boil them until tender. Drain and mash with the butter.

3 Squeeze the pulp of the roasted garlic from each clove and add to the parsnips. Purée the mixture with the cream and seasoning of salt and pepper using the pulse button, so that you end up with a fairly rough texture. Check the seasoning. Reheat in a saucepan and serve.

A dish from northern Italy, where they love their various radicchios. This is a good counterpart for strongly flavored game.

RADICCHIO with red onions

serves 6

2 large heads radicchio

2 red onions, peeled

2 tbsp olive oil

4 tbsp balsamic vinegar

salt and pepper

extra virgin olive oil for serving

1 Halve each head of radicchio, then cut each half into 4 sections. Trim the base and a little of the white heart from each piece, without letting the sections fall apart.

2 Halve the onions and trim the base of each. Cut each half lengthways into crescent-moon-shaped wedges, about ½ inch (1.5cm) wide at their widest part.

3 Heat the olive oil in a frying pan and sauté the onions quickly over a fairly high heat until colored. Turn the heat down low and let the onions cook for about 4 minutes, until they soften. Turn the heat up, add the balsamic vinegar, and, while it's bubbling away, quickly add the radicchio. Let it color on each side—this will happen very quickly—and wilt. Season with salt and pepper and serve with a little extra virgin olive oil drizzled over the top.

Savoy cabbage as it should be—well-seasoned and lightly cooked—and if you've never liked cabbage, this is a revelation. I could eat platefuls of this on its own. It goes admirably with pork, baked ham, game, and roast beef.

SAVOY CABBAGE with garlic and juniper

serves 6

1lb 8oz (675g) Savoy cabbage

8 juniper berries

1 fat garlic clove, peeled

¼ cup (½ stick) butter

salt and pepper

1 Cut the core out of the cabbage and shred the leaves, not too finely (about ¾ inch/2cm thick). Wash. Crush the juniper berries and garlic in a mortar and pestle. Melt the butter in a heavy-bottomed pan and add the cabbage, crushed juniper berries and garlic, salt, pepper, and about 4 tbsp of water. Turn the heat down low, cover the pan, and cook the cabbage for 4 minutes, shaking it vigorously every so often. Stir, so the buttery juices coat the cabbage, and serve immediately.

There are many variations on the red cabbage and fruit theme, but I like the tartness that cranberries bring. This reheats amazingly.

RED CABBAGE with cranberries

serves 8

2 tbsp butter

1 medium red onion, chopped

1 medium red cabbage

1 tart eating apple, peeled, cored, and roughly chopped

3 tbsp balsamic vinegar

2 tbsp brown sugar

1 tsp pumpkin pie spice

1oz (30g) dried cranberries and 3oz (75g) fresh cranberries

salt and pepper

1 Melt the butter in a heavy-bottomed casserole dish and sauté the onion until soft but not colored.

2 Quarter the cabbage, remove the hard central core and discard, and slice the rest finely. Put it in the pot with the onion and all the remaining ingredients. Stir, cover, and cook over a low heat for about half an hour, stirring from time to time. Check the seasoning before serving.

Beets, roasted to a rich, earthy sweetness, are a great partner for tangy goat cheese. The combination is very good in a tart, and here it is used as a wonderful ingredient for a warm salad. I hope this dish will banish forever the specter of beets as they are often used, as a vinegar-laden crimson balls that make your mouth pucker and stains everything else on the plate. It was the cooking of Scandinavia that really turned me on to the beet's potential, though this salad is based on one I had in America.

ROAST BEET SALAD
with orange and goat cheese

serves 6

750g (1lb 10oz) small beet, uncooked

9oz (250g) creamy goat cheese

3 medium-sized oranges

7oz (200g) salad leaves (corn salad lettuce, baby spinach leaves, and watercress)

3oz (75g) walnut halves, toasted

for the dressing:

1 tbsp white wine vinegar

½ tbsp orange juice

small dollop of Dijon mustard

salt and pepper

5 tbsp extra virgin olive oil

½ tsp honey

1 Cook the beet according to the instructions on page 76. Make the dressing by whisking all the ingredients together and break the goat cheese into chunks.

2 Slice the ends off the oranges so that they are flat at the top and bottom. Using a small sharp knife, cut the peel and pith from the fruit, working from top to bottom all the way around. Cut the oranges into fine slices, removing any pips and the little white bits of pith in the center of each slice.

3 It's nice to serve this dish while the beets are still warm, so once cooked, leave until cool enough to handle and then rub or peel the skins off. Cut each beet into quarters. Toss the leaves, oranges, and walnuts with the dressing, retaining about 4 tbsp of dressing. Either split the salad between 6 plates or put it into 1 big shallow bowl. Because beet stain everything they touch, put the beets and the goat cheese on top of the salad after it has been tossed. Drizzle over the remaining dressing and serve immediately.

"Today I think
> *Only with scents—scents dead leaves yield,*
> *And bracken, and wild carrot's seed,*
> *And the square mustard field...."*

DIGGING EDWARD THOMAS

"I love the smell of hunting clothes; the felt was impregnated with scents of the forest, the leaves, the air, and blood…And the oily, metallic smell of the gun. And the raw, sour smell of the leather. I loved all of it."

EMBERS SÁNDOR MÁRAI

TALES FROM THE HUNT
game and wild mushrooms

It took me a while to get used to game. Though country born and bred, I am not from a hunting and shooting family. Game would enter our house as gifts. When my dad arrived home with a handful of pheasants—I was about five years old at the time—their bodies still warm, their eyes beady and open, their feathers beautiful but blotched with markings as dark and mysterious as those of a jungle animal, I screamed the house down. This was real food and it was frightening.

Game is very different to farmed meat. It tastes of the earth, the result of a diet of berries, wild grain, grass, and grubs—no wonder we describe it as "strong". Then there's its dense meat and sinewy body, the effects of a life of hard work and freedom. The cook needs to work respectfully—basting, barding, moistening—to bring the animal to tenderness. Put game in a pot with the time-honored flavorings of wine, onions, and herbs, and you end up with rich, assertive, muscular food. If you've shot the game yourself, you can take added pleasure, similar to dealing with home-grown vegetables, that you've procured your own food: a basic age-old pride that is almost instinctive and links us with the past.

Time spent in France brought me round to the idea of eating game. On exchange programs there in my teens, the men of the house would go off quietly with their guns and be proud of the rabbits they brought back. These rabbits tasted so good—golden fleshed after being pot-roasted in an old casserole dish with bacon, rosemary, and a splash of wine—that it was impossible not to hope their hunts would be successful. My husband goes off to shoot bunnies and pigeons, and his pleasure seems not to be so much in the kill as in the walk and the concentration required. Hunting for, and cooking, game seems entirely natural to me, as long as the hunt is not a booze-fueled bash, in which killing is more important than getting food.

Not all game is truly wild nowadays. In order to maintain stock for organized shoots, pheasants and partridges are bred before being released. Properly wild birds are all types of wild duck, grouse, pigeon, woodcock and snipe. In America, the most common type of game bird is the bobwhite quail, especially in the South. Often it is propagated in captivity and released on hunting reserves, but I'm still fond of the little birds. The flavor may be mild, but quails still make for good eating: there are plenty of small bones to get your chops around, they cook quickly, and they look elegant.

Rabbit, sold both wild and farmed, is also rather looked down on—perhaps because it can never be strong enough for real macho game eaters—but it tastes better than chicken and works with many different flavors. I wish we made more of venison, too. Farmed venison is just as good as the wild stuff as both kinds graze, the farmed animals are not forced to grow at unreasonable rates, and all venison farms hang their meat. In times when much meat tastes bland, fall and winter servings of venison, pheasant, and rabbit shouldn't just be for special occasions, but a regular part of our diet.

When cooking game, the key issue is to stop it from becoming dry. Don't marinate it in a bottle of claret before you start cooking, as so many recipes instruct; the alcohol only draws out moisture. Marinating it in herbs or spices moistened with olive oil is much better. As a rule, cook quickly at a high heat, or long and slow at a very gentle one, larding with fat or cooking it with bacon and basting it often.

There is a machismo to game eating. Many are the stories about pheasant so high it crawled with maggots or parted company with its head as it was hanging, and I've eaten with men so intent on gamey grouse that I could hardly bear to be at the same table. Girly though it may be, I prefer my game subtly flavored. One of the good things about game is that it is not a standardized product. If you buy it from a good butcher or dealer, you have a say in how strong a flavor you want it to have, depending on how long it has been hung.

The hunt for mushrooms is of an entirely different order. It is the silent hunt, and the hiddenness of the hunting ground is one of the great attractions of mushroom picking. Scandinavians talk about secret places, and the French refer to their hunting grounds as "*nids*" or "nests". Fungi are mysterious and magical. These vibrantly colored umbrellas and toadstool-shaped houses peopled with distinctive characters—little brown pigs or *porcini, chanterelles* looking like yellow-skirted ballerinas, mushrooms that resemble little bearded men—inhabit a world of leaves and mulch.

My best mushrooming trips have been in France, leaving with friends first thing in the morning (the best time to pick) with flasks of warm food and wine. We're not too serious, we just want enough mushrooms to fry up that evening, and we take as much pleasure in the environment—the bosky smell in our nostrils and the sun beginning to filter through the trees—as we do in the mushrooms. And yet the hunt gets under your skin. You become completely focused on the mushrooms in a way that is almost meditative.

Porcini, also known as *ceps* and in Great Britain as penny buns, are the kings of mushrooms. With a dark brown cap and a swollen stem, they have the most pronounced meaty flavor. If you're lucky enough to get big ones, grill them whole or bake them, stuffed with breadcrumbs, garlic, and parsley. *Chanterelles* are more delicate creatures, egg-yolk yellow, trumpet-shaped, and with a slight smell of apricots. Both these types of fungi dry well, and there is nothing wrong with replacing wild mushrooms in a recipe with a mixture of dried wild and fresh cultivated ones.

Fresh wild mushrooms are now more available commercially but, since they're not cheap, you'll want to treat them properly. Don't buy any that are slimy, withered, or broken. Clean them with a soft brush and cook them as soon as possible, though a day in the fridge in a paper bag isn't the end of the world. Even a simple sauté has to be done with care. Cook the mushrooms first in a little hot oil, then turn the heat down and add butter for flavor. Mushrooms can throw off a lot of moisture, which is fine if you are making a sauce, but if you want them to be drier, then continue to cook them until the moisture has evaporated. Add a little cream and sherry or Madeira for a sauce to eat with guinea fowl or pasta, make them into one of the most luxurious omelets, or add a little garlic and parsley and serve straight from an old black skillet.

Even the idea of this dish makes me yearn for October, it is so full of strong, sweet autumnal flavors and colors. Instead of roasting pheasant, you could just sauté pheasant breasts, deglaze the pan, and proceed as in the recipe. If you can't get blackberries, then just leave them out—they look lovely but the quinces are great on their own.

ROAST PHEASANT
with quince, blackberries, and honey

serves 4

3 tbsp unsalted butter

2 oven-ready pheasants, about
1lb 3oz (525g) each

salt and pepper

1 quince

¾ cup dry white wine

3 tbsp mild honey such as
wildflower or heather

2 tbsp cider vinegar

2 cups pheasant or strong
chicken stock

2½ tsp superfine sugar

3½oz (100g) blackberries (about
12 good-size blackberries)

1 Preheat the oven to 400°F (200°C). Heat 2 tbsp of the butter in a heavy cooking pot in which the pheasant will sit snugly. Brown the birds all over, season well, and roast in the preheated oven for 35 minutes, basting well every so often with the cooking juices.

2 Quarter the quince and remove the core. Cover with the wine and add 2 tbsp of the honey. Bring to the boil, then turn down the heat to a simmer and cook the quince until tender—about 20 minutes.

3 When the pheasant is cooked, remove it from the pot and keep warm. Pour the fat and cooking juices from the pot into a dish and separate the fat by spooning it off. Discard the fat. Add the remaining honey to the pan and cook until you can just smell it caramelizing; this happens quickly, so be careful. Pour on the vinegar—the mixture will spit a little but don't worry. Add the stock, the cooking liquor from the quince, and the skimmed cooking juices. Reduce until slightly syrupy.

4 Slice the cooked quinces. Melt the rest of the butter in a frying pan, sprinkle on half of the sugar, and cook the slices on both sides just to brown them. Add the blackberries and turn around in the buttery juices to heat a little, adding the rest of the sugar. Be careful not to squash the blackberries or the juices will stain the quinces.

5 Carve or joint the pheasant and serve with a little of the sauce, laying slices of quince and a few blackberries alongside each serving.

I love cooking with marmalade. Its bitter-sweet flavor seems just right for winter, and it gives such a lovely burnished glaze to meat.

STUFFED QUAIL
with marmalade and whiskey

serves 4

½ cup marmalade

8 tbsp whiskey

leaves from 4 sprigs fresh thyme

salt and pepper

8 quails

8 slices bacon, cut in two

1¾ cups very well-flavored chicken stock plus another 2 tbsp whiskey

for the stuffing:

½ small onion, very finely chopped

2 slices bacon, finely chopped

1 tbsp butter

2oz (50g) breadcrumbs

1 tbsp very finely chopped fresh flat-leaf parsley

1 small egg, beaten

1 Mix the marmalade, whiskey, thyme, salt, and pepper together and spoon over the quails. Cover loosely and leave to marinate for anything from 1 hour to overnight.

2 Preheat the oven to 400°F (200°C). Make the stuffing by sautéeing the onion and bacon in the melted butter until golden. Add the breadcrumbs, chopped parsley, egg, salt, and pepper. Stuff each quail with this mixture—it's a sticky process but manageable—and put a crisscross of bacon on top of each bird. Season with pepper. Spoon the marinade over the birds again. Put the birds in a pot in which they will all fit snugly and cover. Cook in the preheated oven for 25 minutes, or until cooked through, spooning the juices and marinade over the birds every so often.

3 While the birds are cooking, reduce the chicken stock by half, or until it is slightly syrupy, and add the whiskey. Check for seasoning—you might want to add some pepper, but you shouldn't need to.

4 Serve 2 quails per person with a little of the sauce spooned around them.

"It snowed all yesterday and never emptied the sky, although the clouds looked so low and heavy they might drop all at once with a thud. The light is diffuse and hueless, like the light on paper inside a pewter bowl....The dark is overhead and the light at my feet; I'm walking upside-down in the sky."

PILGRIM AT TINKER CREEK ANNIE DILLARD

In Austria the old-fashioned dishes are still the most loved. The best place to go for these are the little time-warp restaurants called *beisl* (Yiddish for "little house"); informal eateries with heavy furniture and wooden paneling, full of bustling Viennese matrons and families straight out of *The Sound of Music*. Here you should throw caution to the wind and enjoy such no-nonsense dishes as caraway roast pork with cabbage, bubbling cheese-covered *spätzle,* and apricot dumplings. Old-fashioned *beisl* are so cool these days that new ones are opening. They retain the wood and dark colors of their forebears but serve lighter, more innovative dishes alongside the old stalwarts. I ate this, based on an old-fashioned Styrian *braise*, in Perauer, a new-style *beisl* in Vienna.

STYRIAN VENISON
with chestnuts, cranberries, and wild mushrooms

serves 6

1oz (30g) dried wild mushrooms

1½oz (40g) dried cranberries

3½ cups game or well-flavored chicken stock

4½oz (125g) fresh wild mushrooms, or well-flavored cultivated mushrooms

3½oz (100g) cooked chestnuts

½ cup (1 stick) unsalted butter

¼ cup Port

salt and pepper

6 venison steaks, approx. 1-inch (2–2.5-cm) thick

to serve:

2 tbsp unsalted butter

18 perfectly intact cooked chestnut halves

50g (2oz) fresh cranberries

⅔ cup sour cream

1 Pour enough boiling water over the dried wild mushrooms and cranberries to just cover them and leave them to soak for about 45 minutes. Drain and add the juices to the game or chicken stock. Boil the stock until it has reduced to 1 cup. Slice the fresh mushrooms and quarter the chestnuts. Cut up the larger reconstituted dried mushrooms.

2 Melt ¼ cup butter in a frying pan and add the fresh mushrooms. Sauté briskly for about 4 minutes, then add the chestnuts and cook for another 3 minutes. Deglaze the pan with the port and let the alcohol bubble away. Add the dried mushrooms, cranberries, and stock. Bring to the boil and bubble for a few minutes, until the mixture is slightly syrupy. Season.

3 Just before you want to serve, season the steaks and melt the remaining butter in a frying pan. Sear the meat on both sides over a high heat, then turn the heat down and cook until they are the doneness of rare steak (about 3 minutes on each side).

4 Meanwhile, to serve, quickly melt the butter and sauté the chestnuts until warm and glossy, then add the fresh cranberries and quickly heat those, without allowing them to become mushy. Cut each steak into 4 slices, just to reveal the lovely pinkness inside, spoon the sauce onto the plate alongside the meat, and top the meat with a good dollop of sour cream and the sautéed chestnuts and cranberries.

This beet sauce is a classic accompaniment to game in Russia, so don't feel you should serve it just with partridge. I'm not a big fan of *kasha*—the grain the eastern Europeans often serve with game—as I find the flavor so strong, but a bowl of nutty bulgar wheat is great on the side. Serve a watercress salad, too.

RUSSIAN PARTRIDGE
with beet and sour cream

serves 4

1lb 9oz (700g) beets

2 tbsp unsalted butter

salt and pepper

4 partridges

¼ cup dry white wine

½ onion, finely chopped

1 tbsp salted butter

1 tsp all-purpose flour

⅔ cup sour cream

2 tsp white wine vinegar

1½ tsp sugar

2 tbsp chopped fresh dill

I Preheat the oven to 375°F (190°C). Wash the beets and remove any leaves, cutting them off about 1½ inches (4cm) from the base, but don't do anything more to them. Any further cutting or trimming will make the crimson juices run out while cooking. Wrap the beet in tin foil, place in a small roasting tray and bake until tender. Depending on the size of the beet, this can take anything from 45 minutes to almost 2 hours. Take out of the oven and leave to cool. Turn the oven down to 350°F (180°C).

2 Melt the unsalted butter in a heavy-bottomed pan in which all the partridges will fit snugly. Season the birds inside and out, then brown them on all sides. Add the wine, bring up to a simmer, then cover the pan and cook in the oven for 30–35 minutes, until cooked through. Baste the partridge regularly with the cooking juices.

3 When the beets are cool, peel them and cut into small cubes. Sauté the onion in the butter until soft but not colored. Add the flour and stir for 1 minute. Add the beets, sour cream, vinegar, and sugar, and season. Cook until warmed, adding a little water if the sauce seems too thick. Add the dill and, when the partridge is cooked, serve it with a spoonful of its cooking juices and the beet sauce.

"Snowdrifts had swaddled Voronezh a couple of days before; now the city glittered under a crust of ice. Light streamed from every surface…'It must be about minus twenty, I suppose,' he said, peeling layers of clothing from me. 'The perfect temperature— everything looks wonderful, it's too cold to work, the vodka's chilled by the time it's home from the kiosk…'"

BLACK EARTH CITY CHARLOTTE HOBSON

"From these bare trees
  The sticks of last year's nests
  Print sad characters against the moon;
  While wind-blown moonlight,
  Stripping fields to silver,
  Scrawls December on each frozen pond"
                                    F.R. HIGGINS

This recipe may be Austrian, but you'd be just as likely to find this dish in Russia, Poland, or made with crème fraîche instead of sour cream, in France. It's one of those simple but classic game recipes that has been on the go for years and will keep on going. The cooking time is for wild rabbit, which is stronger in flavor than the tame beast, but if you prefer the more delicate farmed stuff, halve the cooking time.

AUSTRIAN RABBIT
with bacon and sour cream

serves 4

1oz (30g) dried wild mushrooms

2 tbsp unsalted butter

salt and pepper

8 rabbit pieces

5½oz (150g) bacon in-the-piece, cut into chunks about ½ inch (1cm) square

1 large onion, roughly chopped

2 tsp all-purpose flour

⅔ cup dry white wine

1¼ cups well-flavored chicken stock

2 bay fresh leaves

3 sprigs fresh thyme

1¼ cups sour cream

1 Pour enough boiling water over the dried mushrooms to just cover and leave to soak for 15 minutes. Meanwhile, melt the butter in a heavy-bottomed casserole dish, season the rabbit, and gently cook on all sides until golden. You want to get a bit of color on the outside, not to cook it through. Remove the meat and set it aside.

2 In the same pan, sauté the bacon until golden on all sides, then add the onion and cook until soft but not colored. Stir in the flour and mix well, then add the wine, stock, and the soaking liquor from the mushrooms. Cut up any mushrooms that are very large and add these to the pan with the whole mushrooms. Bring up to the boil, then turn down to a simmer and put the rabbit back in. Add the herbs and season. Cook gently, uncovered, on a low heat until the rabbit is almost cooked through and the liquid has reduced—this takes about 1 hour 10 minutes, but check the rabbit before this time. It is ready when it is tender but still moist and no longer bloody near the bone.

3 Whisk in the sour cream and let the dish cook for 5 minutes, but don't let it boil. Serve with thick egg noodles such as tagliatelle.

Unashamedly old-fashioned, you can make men fall in love with you with this pie. It seems to have even greater seductive powers than a good cleavage.

BEEF PIE
with wild mushrooms and claret

serves 6

1oz (30g) dried wild mushrooms

peanut oil

2lb 4oz (1kg) chuck roast, cut into large chunks, or stew beef

12oz (350g) shallots

¼ cup (½ stick) butter

1 celery stalk, finely chopped

2 garlic cloves, crushed

salt and pepper

¼ cup all-purpose flour

1 cup red wine

leaves from 3 sprigs fresh thyme

3 bay leaves

10½oz (300g) fresh mushrooms, cleaned and sliced

3 tbsp finely chopped parsley

1lb (450g) puff pastry for 1 big pie, 1lb 5oz (600g) for 6 small ones

1 egg, beaten

1 Pour enough boiling water over the dried mushrooms to just cover. Leave to soak.

2 Heat 2 tbsp of the oil in a heavy-bottomed casserole dish and brown the meat really well on all sides. Remove and set aside. Add the peeled green onions to the pan and lightly brown them, adding a little more oil if you need to. Turn the heat down, add 1½ tbsp of the butter, and all the celery and garlic and sweat for 5 minutes. Add the meat, with any juices that have leached out, back to the casserole dish. Season well and, on a low heat, add the flour. Stir everything round until it is well coated. Cut up the wild mushrooms and add these to the pot with their soaking liquid. Add the red wine, thyme, and bay leaves and bring to the boil. Cover and cook on a very gentle heat for 1½ hours, stirring every so often. Take the cover off the pan for the last 15 minutes to reduce the cooking liquid.

3 Melt the remaining butter in a frying pan and cook the fresh mushrooms over a fairly high heat so that they get well coloured. Season and let the mushrooms cook until they exude their liquid and it evaporates.

4 Preheat the oven to 425°F (220°C). Stir the parsley and the cooked fresh mushrooms into the meat and check the seasoning. Put the meat in 1 large or 6 small pie dishes and roll out the pastry. Cut a strip or strips large enough to go around the edge of the pie dish or dishes. Brush the edge of the dish with water and press the pastry strip on to it. Dampen this with water and cover the pie or pies, pressing the pastry down. Trim off the excess, knock up the edges, and crimp. Use the remaining pastry to decorate. Brush with beaten egg and chill for half an hour. Bake in the preheated oven for 35–40 minutes for 1 large pie, 25–30 for smaller ones. Serve immediately.

The Swedes—and the Finns and the Norwegians—are mushroom crazy and often pair them with their beloved fish. I found versions of this dish made with turbot and the European flatfish brill as well as halibut, sometimes topped with chopped, still-warm boiled egg and dill, or warm shrimps.

This is a gloriously simple dish, full of the clean flavors that distinguish Scandinavian cookery, and brings together the woods and the sea. You do need fresh horseradish root for it.

SWEDISH HALIBUT
with wild mushrooms and horseradish

serves 4

9oz (250g) fresh wild mushrooms, or a mixture of wild and cultivated mushrooms

4 x 6oz (175g) filets of halibut

all-purpose flour, seasoned with salt and pepper

½ cup (1 stick) butter

2 tbsp dry white wine

salt and pepper

1 tbsp finely chopped fresh flat-leaf parsley

1½oz (40g) grated fresh horseradish

1 Carefully clean the mushrooms. Cut large ones in half or quarters, but leave the small ones whole.

2 Dip the filets of fish in the seasoned flour. Heat 2 tbsp of the butter in a frying pan and in it cook the fish over a medium heat for about 1½ minutes on each side. Leave the fish skin-side-down, pour on the wine, turn the heat down, and cover the pan. Leave the filets to cook for about 4 minutes in the steam created by the liquid, until they are opaque and cooked through.

3 Meanwhile, melt ½ stick butter in another frying pan and cook the mushrooms briskly until colored. Season and add the parsley.

4 Melt the rest of the butter. Put a filet of fish on each plate, spoon the mushrooms around, and drizzle the melted butter over each serving. Finally top each piece of fish with the horseradish and serve immediately.

Talk to my Polish friend, Kasia, about pierogi and she is practically on the next flight to Warsaw. They are stuffed dumplings made from noodle dough and virtually anything can go inside them: bacon, cabbage, cheese, meat, wild mushrooms, even cherries, for a sweet version. These are also good with bits of fried bacon and warmed sour cream.

POTATO PIEROGI
with wild mushrooms

serves 4

for the noodle dough:

yolks from 2 large eggs plus 10 tbsp water

2 cups all-purpose flour

1 tsp salt

1 tbsp sunflower or vegetable oil

1 egg white, lightly beaten

for the potato filling:

3 tbsp butter

1 medium onion, finely chopped

1lb 2oz (500g) mashing potatoes, such as Yukon Gold, peeled

4½oz (125g) ricotta

2oz (50g) feta, crumbled finely

2 tbsp freshly grated Parmesan

salt and pepper

for the sauce:

⅓ cup (5½ tbsp) unsalted butter

14oz (400g) wild mushrooms, or wild and cultivated, cleaned

salt and pepper

¾ cup each of sour cream and heavy cream

1 For the dough, add half the water to the egg yolks and beat lightly. Add this to the flour and salt and blend, then add the oil and the rest of the water. Bring everything together into a ball. Wrap in plastic wrap and chill for 30 minutes.

2 To make the filling, melt the butter and sauté the onion in it until soft but not colored. Cook the potatoes in salted water until tender. Drain, mash really well, and add the onion with all the buttery juices. Mix in the other ingredients and season well.

3 Split the dough in half and, dealing with one piece at a time, roll out on a lightly floured surface to about 1⁄16 inch (2mm) thick. The dough must be thin, but not so thin that it will tear and lose the filling. Cut circles 3¼ inches (8cm) in diameter. Gather up the remainder of the pastry and roll it out again and cut more circles out of this. Moisten the edges of each dough circle with the beaten egg white and place a little filling in the middle. Press one half over to meet the other and seal. Finish each one by pressing the edges with the tines of a fork. Keep on a floured baking sheet until you're ready to cook them.

4 Bring a very large saucepan of water to the boil—the dumplings need a lot of room to circulate without sticking to each other—then turn it down to a simmer. Add the pierogi and cook for 7 minutes.

5 To make the sauce, melt the butter in a frying pan until foaming, then add the mushrooms. Sauté briskly to get a good color, then continue to cook so the mushrooms throw off some of their moisture. Season well and add the creams. Heat through, but don't let the sauce boil or it will split. Drain the pierogi and serve with the sauce on top.

These make the prettiest and most luxurious starter or side dish. It's difficult to be exact about quantities as it depends on the size of the squash you use, so you may need more cream than suggested.

ROAST WINTER SQUASH
with porcini cream

serves 4 as a side dish

2 small winter squash or pumpkin, such as sweet dumpling or butternut

¾–1oz (20–30g) dried porcini mushrooms

butter, softened

salt and pepper

½–1 cup heavy cream

1–1½oz (30–40g) Parmesan, freshly grated

1 Halve the squash and scoop out the fiber and seeds. Just cover the dried mushrooms with boiling water and leave to soak for 15 minutes. Preheat the oven to 375°F (190°C).

2 Place the squash in a roasting tray and smear butter on the inside and around the flesh at the top. Season. Drain the mushrooms and divide them between the squash halves. Pour cream into the cavity and season again. Cook in the preheated oven for 30–45 minutes, or until completely tender. You may need to top up with cream if you are using a squash that takes a particularly long time to cook. Divide the cheese between each squash about 15 minutes before the end of cooking time.

"*Heap high the groaning platter with pink*
  filets, sucking pig and thick gammon, celestial chef. Be generous with
  the crackling. Let your hand slip with the gravy trough, dispensing plenty."

AN ODE TO ENGLISH FOOD GEORGE MACBETH

THE FAT OF THE LAND
pork

Pork is the meat I most associate with winter. Its succulent fattiness keeps out the cold, and the dishes we cook with it are satisfying and gutsy rather than refined. Its closest companions—apples, dried fruit, beans and lentils, mustard, juniper, cabbage, caraway seeds, and maple syrup—are also good fall and winter ingredients. If you have these to hand and a good source of well-bred pork, an old-fashioned feast is never far away.

We love pork's sweet fattiness, its almost gamey taste and the joy of salty crackling. The American and European canon of classic dishes is one long line of porkers: rough country pâtés and pork filet with prunes in France; poached Italian sausage with beans and *mostarda*; loin of pork studded with caraway seeds and served with sauerkraut in Austria; sweet-glazed spare ribs in the U.S., and roast pork with apple sauce in Great Britain and Ireland. And across Europe there are more hams, sausages, and salamis than you ever thought possible.

Pigs are like humans: gregarious yet independent, with a desire to be surrounded by companions and hungry for any food that is put in front of them. Their IQ is on a par with that of dogs. They can be taught to perform tasks such as truffle hunting and can recognize their owners. Few animals arouse such feelings in farmers and much has been written about the difficulty of slaughtering family pigs that are regarded as pets. Tomi Ungerer, in his book *Far Out Isn't Far Enough*, an account of his time spent on a small homestead in rural Nova Scotia, writes that pig killing was a popular topic of conversation among neighbors, but that it was considered bad luck, even rude, to use the word "pig". The pig was more commonly referred to as "Mr. Dennis", so someone might comment: "My mother, when we killed Mr. Dennis, she locked herself in the house and played the harmonium." We get emotional about pigs, perhaps because they remind us of ourselves.

Pigs are now raised and slaughtered all year round, but in the past (and even now in some parts of Europe) the autumnal pig killing day was a cause for celebration and feasting. The day of slaughter is mystical. The more carefully nurtured the pig, the greater the joy at eating and using every part, and the hams and salami that result feed country families all through the winter. Thus the pig is considered special.

But most of the pork we eat comes from pigs that have been raised under intensive methods. In much modern pig farming, these sociable creatures are not allowed to roam or forage for food outside, as is their natural wont, but are confined to such small areas that the company of others is a torment. They get depressed, which shows itself in bar biting and injuries, particularly to the ears and tail, are common as the pigs get stressed.

As well as being cruel, this kind of farming produces meat that is flabby and tasteless. Instead of the varied diet they naturally prefer, factory-farmed pigs are fed on the same food pellets every day, are reared to grow fast, and, because of the risk of infection due to the close confines in which they live, can be filled with antibiotics. Modern pig breeds have also been bred to have less fat, thus removing one of the main providers of succulence and flavor. But we don't have to eat pork like this. With more small farmers looking for quality and flavor, it is possible to source pork that at least has an organic label, thus ensuring better animal welfare. Find pork that has been reared humanely, allowed to graze, and given a varied diet by a caring farmer. If from one of the "rare breed" pigs, then you're doing even better. If your butcher can tell you how the pork he or she sells has been reared and what breed it is, treasure that butcher and be happy to pay the price asked for this superior meat. Otherwise, find a farm where you can source your pork directly and don't let your buying standards drop when you're looking for bacon, ham, or sausages.

We tend to be a bit unadventurous when it comes to cooking pork, sticking to the ubiquitous pork chop, perhaps because we are confused about which cuts should be used for what. As far as fresh pork goes, the best cuts for roasting are the loin and leg. The shoulder, a cheaper cut, is great for slow-roasting, and the belly, with its lovely layering of fat, produces an exquisitely sweet mouthful and great crackling. It can also be boned and stuffed and is the cut that provides spare ribs and the meat for pork terrines and pâtés. Salted, it is what the French serve in slices with lentils and mustard sauce to make the bistro classic, *petit salé*.

Pork filet is completely lean and needs to be cooked quickly, either by roasting (though it needs copious basting), or sautéed in medallions or escalopes. One of my mother's best dishes is pork escalopes battered with a mallet, coated with egg and breadcrumbs and fried—delicious with sautéed potatoes and a good dollop of English mustard. Chops can be cut from the loin but are even tastier if they're from the shoulder joint as they have good marbling (theses are known as spare-rib chops). The knuckle or hock is cheap and largely overlooked. Fresh, salted, or smoked, it's wonderfully gelatinous and hits the bliss spot when cooked slowly and served with lentils or beans.

Hams are made from the hind leg and are cured by salting and drying, and sometimes smoking as well, and come in two forms: one that is "raw" but ready-to-eat, such as Parma ham, and one that requires further cooking, such as the ham that, glazed with sugar and mustard and studded with cloves, often adorns the Christmas or Easter table. Bacon, which comes from the back or the belly of the pig, is also cured and can be smoked. Quite a few of the recipes in this book call for Speck. In Germany this just means bacon, but in Austria and northern Italy it is boned pork flank that has been cured in juniper berries, garlic and sugar, dried, and then smoked. There is nothing quite like it for a good, strong, spicy pork flavor.

Coming downstairs to the smell of frying bacon is one of the best starts to the day. When staying at my grandparents' farm when I was a child, the morning always began with my granny making potato bread at the kitchen table and thick rashers of bacon spitting on the stove. If we are demanding about the pork we eat, a good breakfast like this will remain a reality, not a nostalgic food memory.

This is basically Swedish hash, and the end result is a lot better than you'd expect from just reading the ingredients list. It's a real hunger-stopper, and a great example of a home-cooked dish that has lasted. *Pytt i panna* was originally devised to use up leftovers from the Sunday roast dinner, but people now make it from scratch and put all sorts of meat into it. I like to include some lightly smoked meat or sausage. Traditionally, it's served with a raw egg yolk, but many people prefer it topped with a whole fried egg. Serve with sweet pickled beet or cucumber (see the sweet pickled cucumber on page 91). Great with a glass of ice-cold Scandinavian lager.

PYTT I PANNA
Swedish hash

serves 4

1lb 5oz (600g) potato, peeled

3 tbsp butter

3 tbsp sunflower or vegetable oil

2 onions, finely chopped

2 tbsp chopped fresh flat-leaf parsley

salt and pepper

14oz (400g) cooked meat, a mixture of roast pork, bacon, and sausage

4 eggs

1 Cut the potato into very neat cubes, just over ½ inch (1cm) square. Heat 2 tbsp of the butter and 1 tbsp sunflower oil in one pan, and 1 tbsp butter and another 1 tbsp of oil in another. Sauté the potatoes in the first pan and the onions in the second.

2 Once the potatoes are colored, cover the pan and continue to cook until soft. Both the onions and the potatoes should be soft and golden. Add the onions to the potatoes, throw in the parsley, and season. Cover while you cook the meat.

3 Heat another 1 tbsp of oil in the pan used for the onions and quickly sauté the cooked meat. Add to the potato. Fry 4 eggs in a little more oil. Serve the *pytt i panna* immediately with a fried egg on top of each serving.

"Tout est bon dans un cochon"
"Everything about the pig tastes good"
GRIMOD DE LE REYNIERE ALMANACH DES GOURMANDS

While researching a book on British and Irish dining pubs, I fell in love with pork and realized how much you could do with it. A salad based on the great British fried breakfast might not seem promising, but it's a knockout. Try to buy your blood sausage (or black pudding, as it's known in Great Britain) from good butcher's stores as it will be fresher and full of flavor.

FARMER'S SALAD

serves 6

12oz (350g) waxy potatoes

6oz (175g) blood sausage

10½oz (300g) pancetta or bacon, cut into ⅔ inch (1.5cm) cubes

6 tbsp olive or peanut oil for frying

salt and pepper

6oz (175g) salad leaves

6 large eggs

for the dressing:

4 tbsp extra virgin olive oil

½ tbsp balsamic vinegar

1 tsp honey grain-mustard

1 garlic clove, crushed

I Cook the potatoes in simmering water until just tender. Drain and, when they are cool enough to handle, peel. Cut into slices about ¼ inch (5mm) thick. Make the dressing by whisking the oil into the other ingredients. Season.

2 Remove the skin from the blood sausage and cut into rounds about ⅓ inch (1cm) thick. Heat 1 tbsp oil and sauté the blood sausage and bacon until they are colored and cooked through. At the same time, in a different pan, sauté the potatoes in another 2 tbsp oil until golden on each side. Season well.

3 Toss everything, except the eggs, with the dressing, being careful not to break up the potatoes. Quickly fry the eggs in another 3 tbsp of oil. Divide the salad between 6 plates and top each with a fried egg. Serve immediately.

"The pudding's purple,
Flecked with white, blackens as you turn it
Until it shines with fat, a winning set
Of draughts."

BLACK PUDDING JOHN FULLER

This was the first dish I ever ate in Scandinavia. I'd just arrived—very late—from the airport, there was a blizzard outside and this was brought on a candlelit tray by room service in my Copenhagen hotel. What an introduction.

DANISH ROAST PORK
with pickled prunes and sweet cucumber

serves 6–8

1 tbsp fennel seeds

1 tbsp coriander seeds

coarse sea salt and pepper

sunflower or canola oil

3lb 5oz (1.5kg) pork belly, rind scored in a diamond pattern

2 cups dry white wine

for the pickled prunes:

1 cup white wine vinegar

1½ cups superfine sugar

1 stick cinnamon, broken

6 juniper berries, crushed

6 black peppercorns

2 garlic cloves

1lb 2oz (500g) prunes (good-quality, unpitted)

for the cucumber:

1 medium cucumber

3 tsp coarse sea salt

1 tbsp rice wine vinegar

1½ tbsp superfine sugar

1 tbsp chopped fresh dill

1 Make the prunes at least a day ahead. Heat the wine vinegar with the sugar and spices, stirring a little to help the sugar melt. Once it has melted, boil until the liquid has reduced by a third and is quite syrupy. Put the prunes in a sterilized preserving jar (wash it in boiling water and then leave in a low oven for 15 minutes) and pour over the syrup. Cover and leave to plump up.

2 For the pickled cucumber, cut the ends off the cucumber and slice very fine. The slices should be almost transparent. Layer in a colander with the salt, place a plate on top, and set over a bowl so that the cucumber juices can run out. Leave for a couple of hours. Mix the cucumber with the rest of the ingredients and keep covered, until you are ready to serve. (I sometimes skip the salting if I'm in a hurry, in which case you should mix the sliced cucumber with the vinegar and flavorings and serve immediately. It's not as good but it's better than not having them at all.)

3 For the pork, crush the spices with some salt with a mortar and pestle. Add 2 tbsp oil, then rub this all over the flesh of the pork. Cover and refrigerate for an hour.

4 Preheat the oven to 425°F (220°C). Rub the skin of the pork outside with more oil, then season all over with salt and pepper, pressing the salt flakes into the skin. Roast in the preheated oven for 30 minutes.

5 Pour half the white wine around the pork and reduce the heat to 325°F (170°C). Cook for a further 1¼ hours, pouring the rest of the wine around the pork about half an hour before the end of cooking time. Take the pork out of the oven, cover with tin foil, insulate well and leave to rest for about 15 minutes. Carve and serve with the cooking juices and pickled prunes and cucumbers.

Here is another recipe inspired by some of the fantastic cooking in Britain's best dining pubs. I ate a dish like this on a bitterly cold day in the Yorkshire Dales, though it makes me think of Austrian food as much as British fare, especially when I serve it (as I often do) with Savoy cabbage cooked with caraway seeds. Shoulder of pork is a cheap cut that gains a melting texture when cooked slowly.

ROAST PORK WITH BLOOD SAUSAGE,
apple, and mustard sauce

serves 8

5-lb (2.25-kg) boned shoulder of pork, skin scored in a diamond pattern

olive oil

coarse sea salt and pepper

for the stuffing:

7oz (200g) blood sausage, skin removed

1 tbsp butter

1 small tart eating apple, peeled, cored, and cut into small chunks

leaves from 2 sprigs thyme

for the mustard sauce:

1 tbsp butter

4 shallots, finely chopped

¼ cup white wine vinegar

⅔ cup dry white wine

1 cup heavy cream

2 tbsp Dijon mustard

squeeze lemon

1 Preheat the oven to 310°F (160°C).

2 To make the stuffing, cut the blood sausage up roughly. Melt the butter in a frying pan and sauté the pudding until lightly colored. Mix with the apple and thyme and season with salt and pepper.

3 Open out the pork like a book and cut into the thickest part so that it can be opened out further. This just gives you more room to get the stuffing in. Season the inside of the pork with salt and pepper and lay the stuffing on it. Roll up and tie the joint at 1¼ inch (3cm) intervals with string. Rub the meat with olive oil and season well with salt and pepper.

4 Cook the meat in the preheated oven for 4 hours, basting every so often. Take out of the oven and put onto a heated platter. Cover with tin foil, insulate well and allow the pork to rest for about 20 minutes before carving.

5 You can either make the mustard sauce now or in advance. Melt the butter in a small pan and gently sauté the shallots until soft. Add the white wine vinegar, turn up the heat, and boil to reduce to practically nothing. Add the dry white wine and reduce by half, then add the cream, mustard, and a squeeze of lemon. Season with salt and pepper and heat through. The cream sauce will thicken without reducing it further because of the lemon juice. If it is too thick, just add water until you get the consistency you want (it should be about the consistency of heavy cream). Check for seasoning and serve with the pork.

Pork and shellfish is recognized as a successful combination in many cuisines—the saltiness of pork perfectly complementing the sweetness of shellfish. Scallops with bacon and pea purée has become something of a summer classic in Great Britain and Ireland, and this is the fall version. Get really sweet, fat scallops and good-quality bacon.

SEARED SCALLOPS
with bacon and Jerusalem artichoke purée

serves 6

4½oz (125g) bacon in one piece, cut into chunky lardons

18 fresh, fat scallops, cleaned, roes intact

2 tbsp olive oil

salt and pepper

good squeeze lemon

2 tbsp finely chopped fresh flat-leaf parsley

watercress or flat-leaf parsley (optional), to serve

for the artichoke purée:

1lb 2oz (500g) Jerusalem artichokes

good squeeze lemon

⅔ cup heavy cream

salt and white pepper

2 tbsp extra virgin olive oil

a little light chicken stock or water

1 Peel the artichokes, slice them, cover them with water, add a good squeeze of lemon (this stops them from discoloring) and bring to the boil. Simmer until tender.

2 Drain the artichokes and put them back in the pan with the cream. Heat, season with salt and pepper, then purée the mixture in a blender, adding the olive oil as you go. You may find that you need to add a little stock or water as well, but remember that you are not making soup. Once the mixture has cooled, you can keep it in the fridge and gently reheat it later.

3 Cook the scallops and bacon just before serving. In one frying pan, cook the bacon in its own fat, which runs as it is heated. In another, heat the olive oil. (If you have let the artichoke purée cool, you need to heat it in a separate saucepan just before serving and spoon a puddle of it into the middle of each of 6 heated plates.) When the olive oil is really hot, season the scallops with salt and pepper and quickly sear them on each side for about 20 seconds. The time will depends on the thickness of the scallops; you want them to be just cooked through and meltingly tender.

4 Squeeze some fresh lemon over the scallops in the pan, add the parsley, and divide them between the plates of artichoke purée, pouring a drizzle of the hot pan juices on top of each helping. Scatter with the hot bacon. You may want to garnish each plate with a little handful of lightly dressed watercress or a sprig of flat-leaf parsley, before serving.

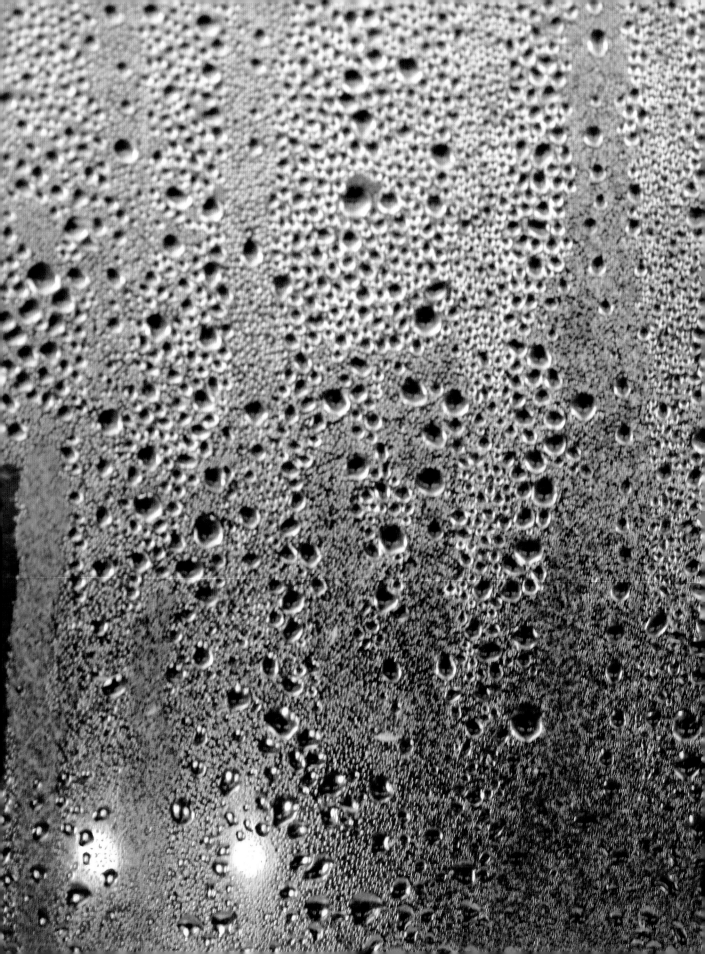

This delicious pasta dish from the Austrian ski slopes is not for those on a diet. The quantity of sour cream called for is not a misprint, so it's best to restrict *schinkenfleckerl* to those freezing days when you've done plenty of physical activity. You can use plain cheese only—Cheddar or Parmesan or a mixture of both—instead of smoked cheese if you prefer. Speck is the German word for bacon, but in both Austria and northern Italy it is boned pork flank that is cured with juniper berries and sugar and aged, and ideally this is what you need for this recipe. Serve with a plain green salad—watercress or baby spinach—on the side.

SCHINKENFLECKERL
Austrian pasta with Speck and smoked cheese

serves 6–8

2 tbsp butter, softened, plus extra for greasing

2 large eggs, 1 of them separated

2½ cups sour cream

14oz (400g) Speck, bacon, or cooked ham, cut into ¾ inch (2cm) chunks

1lb 2oz (500g) fresh pasta, either shapes or noodles such as tagliatelle

5½oz (150g) smoked cheese, grated

1oz (30g) Parmesan, grated

salt and pepper

I Preheat the oven to 375°F (190°C). Cream the butter in a large bowl, then add 1 whole egg and 1 yolk and gradually stir in the sour cream. If you are using Speck or bacon, sauté it in its own fat. Put the pasta on to cook in boiling water.

2 Beat the egg white until it reaches the medium peak stage. Fold this into the egg and cream mixture and add the meat too.

3 Drain the pasta and add to the rest of the ingredients in the bowl. Stir in half the cheese. Season really well with salt and pepper and spoon into a buttered gratin dish. Put the rest of the cheese on top and bake in the preheated oven for about 20 minutes. The top should be nicely browned and slightly souffléed. Serve immediately.

OK, I know this dish sounds unpromising, but when you take your coddle out of the oven you will be just dying to pour yourself a Guinness and tuck in.

DUBLIN CODDLE

serves 4–6

1 tbsp butter

1 tbsp peanut oil

8 good-quality pork sausages

8 slices thickly sliced Canadian bacon

3 onions, thinly sliced

1lb 2oz (800g) potatoes, peeled

4 tbsp chopped flat-leaf parsley

3 cups chicken stock or water

1 Preheat the oven to 350°F (180°C). Heat the butter and oil in a pan and brown the sausages on all sides. Set aside. Quickly color the bacon in the same pan. Set that aside too. Cook the sliced onions, again in the same pan, until just softening and coloring slightly. Slice the potatoes.

2 Layer all the ingredients in a casserole dish, sprinkling with 3 tbsp of the parsley and some salt and pepper as you go. Bring the stock or water (or you could use alcoholic cider if you prefer) to the boil, pour over the ingredients in the casserole dish and cover. Cook in the preheated oven for 1 hour, removing the lid for the last 15 minutes. Scatter on the remaining parsley just before serving.

This dish is both earthy and elegant, and the muskiness of truffle oil gives it a luxurious sexiness.

SALAD OF CURED HAM with truffle oil

serves 6

1lb 10oz (750g) waxy potatoes

1lb 2oz (500g) leeks

1 shallot, very finely sliced

2 tbsp roughly chopped fresh flat-leaf parsley

6 tbsp olive oil

juice of ½ small lemon

salt and pepper

12 thin slices Parma or other cured ham

about 6 tbsp truffle oil

1 Clean the potatoes (but don't peel them) and cook them in salted water until tender.

2 Trim the leeks, discarding the rougher green parts. Cut into chunks about 1½ inches (3cm) long and wash thoroughly. Cook in boiling, salted water for 6 minutes, or until tender (it partly depends on the thickness of the leeks). Drain really well. Drain the potatoes and cut into slices about ¼ inch (5mm) thick. Put the potatoes and leeks into a bowl and add the sliced shallots, chopped parsley, olive oil, and lemon juice. Season.

3 Toss everything together gently. Divide between 6 plates and lay 2 slices of Parma or cured ham on top of each serving. Drizzle the truffle oil over the top and serve immediately.

"...*Laura ran to the block where Pa chopped wood,* and filled her apron with
the fresh, sweet-smelling chips....Instead of burning quickly, the green
chips smouldered and filled the hollow log with thick, choking smoke.
Pa shut the door, and a little smoke squeezed through the crack
around it, and a little smoke came through the roof, but most of it was
shut in with the meat. 'There's nothing better than a good hickory
smoke,' Pa said. 'That will make good venison that will keep
anywhere, in any weather.'"

LITTLE HOUSE IN THE BIG WOODS LAURA INGALLS WILDER

OF WOOD AND SMOKE
smoked food

As children, we used to visit Dublin a couple of times a year, and our first stop was the Wicklow Hotel, all green-shaded lights and deep leather chairs. We thought it was terribly grand, not least because we tucked into smoked salmon as soon as we arrived. The salmon at the Wicklow was perfumed with peat and sliced thicker than normal and was served with a plateful of crumbly wheaten bread. We felt we were eating something truly special and getting a taste of the Irish countryside.

Nowadays, we don't always appreciate smoked foods as much as we should, partly because smoked salmon has become so devalued. It used to be a treat, not a staple whipped out at every minor celebration. We would often source it somewhere special too, instead of wading through supermarket shelves of slippery dyed stuff to try and find a pack worth having. But as long as you can find a quality product, smoked food is a joy and can relieve the cook of having to cook at all. Little halved boiled potatoes, still warm and topped with a daub of sour cream, a sliver of smoked salmon, and a spoonful of keta (salmon roe) is one of the best accompaniments to drinks I can think of. An abundant platter of smoked fish is still decadently luxurious and breathes of the sea and salt. You don't have to stick just to smoked salmon, either. Smoked prawns and mussels are knockout; they aren't easy to come by, but speciality gourmet shops with their own meat and fish counters may be able to help.

Smoked mackerel is somewhat debased in Great Britain, but I suspect that's because it's easy to find in the supermarket. The plump bodies—so burnished you'd think they'd been gilded—for sale at the fish market in Bergen, Norway, are a different kettle of fish: sweet and succulent and in no way a cheap alternative to smoked salmon. Search out the good stuff.

People tend to be frightened of smoked eel, presumably because they are queasy about the live creature's slitheriness, but it provides a lovely, buttery mouthful and is rich enough to be eaten in the simplest way, with brown bread, lemon, and horseradish cream. Indeed, there are wonderful accompaniments to all kinds of smoked fish: horseradish and apple cream; the dilled sour cream of Scandinavia; and the apple, beet, and horseradish relishes so redolent of eastern European cooking.

Since it requires cooking, smoked haddock has a different appeal. Honey-colored and smelling of misty afternoons, it's more of a fancy dinner food. You can turn out a plethora of old-fashioned dishes with it— kedgeree, fish cakes and fish pie—and I like it with the slatey earthiness of Puy lentils and a creamy mustard sauce. It's not bad with parsley sauce either, and it makes a great gratin, layered with potatoes and wild mushrooms. I also like it warm in a salad, tossed with spinach leaves and a mustard dressing and topped with a poached egg. If you're feeling lazy but greedy, you can just bake smoked haddock, skinned and fileted, with wilted spinach and slithers of tomato under a blanket of cream and grated Cheddar: a blissful dinner for a cold Saturday night.

Smoking, presumably discovered by accident when someone realized that meat left hanging in a smoke-filled cave kept longer than normal, is no longer used to preserve food. Now, with fridges and vacuum-packing, we don't need this aspect but we still buy smoked food for its flavor and, I suspect, because we are intrigued and enchanted by the fact that such an ancient way of treating food is still practiced. You only have to spend half an hour in a small smokery, with its tarry walls and woody smells, to want to eat this food.

The smoking process is relatively simple. First the food is salted, either with dry salt or in a brine, which reduces the water content and firms the flesh as well as seasoning it. Then the food is smoked over smoldering hard woods, most commonly oak, beech, birch, and hickory, though aromatic woods such as juniper and apple are sometimes burned in the final stages. Tarry deposits from the smoke are left on the food that, with the salt already absorbed, help kill the bacteria that would otherwise make the food spoil.

Cold-smoking is the most common form of the craft found in Great Britain. With this method, the food (usually fish, though fillet of beef is also treated this way) is smoked at a temperature not higher than 85°F (29°C), so the food is not cooked. The end results can be eaten raw, like smoked salmon, or may require further cooking, like smoked haddock. In hot-smoking, which is much more common in Scandinavia, the food undergoes an initial period of cold-smoking to get the smoky flavor, then the temperature is raised (to between 180°F/82°C and 200°F/93°C for fish and up to 240°F/115°C for poultry and meat) to cook it fully. Hot-smoked salmon, lusciously rich without being cloying, is as common as cold-smoked salmon in Scandinavia and is becoming more common in Great Britain, too. It can be served cold—it's wonderful in a salad with warm potatoes and roast beets, dressed with nothing more than buttermilk, dill, and seasoning— but people also reheat it. I've eaten warm hot-smoked salmon on creamed spinach—a classic Swedish dish —in the covered market in Stockholm at Christmas: a properly celebratory meal for the time of year.

Hot-smoking is even more exciting when applied to chicken, game, and pork. These products are still hard to find, and expensive, but hot-smoking meat is probably the easiest thing for the home-smoker to do. You can experiment with the home-smoking kits on the market, or customize a clean metal garbage can. Whole chickens and breasts of duck, pheasant, and goose are the simplest things to smoke and they open up a world of dishes, most of them easy and quick to put together. A salad of smoked duck and walnuts, dressed with nut oil sweetened with a little cassis, provides a sublime taste of southwest France. Smoked pheasant is lovely with lentils and a creamy garlic dressing. Smoked goose breast, which I came across time and time again in northern Italy, is deliciously earthy served with leaves and drizzled with truffle oil. In Denmark, smoked pork loin is partnered with horseradish cream and lengths of sweet-and-sour rhubarb.

If you don't want to do hot-smoking yourself, you can find smoked chicken quite easily (buy the whole birds rather than the pre-sliced breasts), but you'll have to search for smoked game in small smokeries. This quest for unfamiliar, smoke-infused ingredients is worth the hunt.

I don't usually like inauthentic dishes that fuse a technique from one country's cuisine with ingredients from another, but occasionally it works, and it does here. I'd even expect Italians to like this. Try not to break the smoked haddock up too much—you want to find chunks of it among the rice, not tiny flakes.

SMOKED HADDOCK AND LEEK RISOTTO

serves 4–6

¼ cup (½ stick) butter

4 medium leeks, finely sliced

1lb (450g) smoked haddock, or if you can't get hold of any try smoked trout or whitefish instead

4¼ cups light chicken stock

10½oz (300g) arborio rice

3oz (75g) Parmesan, freshly grated

I Melt the butter in a saucepan and sweat the leeks in it for 15 minutes. Remove any skin from the fish and poach it in a separate saucepan for about 5 minutes in enough simmering chicken stock to cover it. When cooked, leave covered with the stock so it stays moist.

2 Add the rice to the leeks, stir, and cook for about a minute, making sure the rice is well coated with the buttery juices. Have the rest of your stock simmering and start adding it, a ladleful at a time, stirring constantly. Don't add any new liquid until each ladleful has been absorbed. The rice will become sticky and creamy as it cooks and should take about 20 minutes to become soft while retaining a little bite in the center. Use the stock in which the fish has been poached for the final addition of liquid.

3 Gently break the fish into chunks and stir it into the risotto at the last minute, along with 2 tbsp of Parmesan.

4 Check the seasoning—it's unlikely to need salt because of the saltiness of the cheese and fish, but a good grind of black pepper will just finish it off. Serve immediately with the remaining Parmesan.

A platter of smoked fish is still decadently luxurious. Smoked mussels and prawns aren't that easy to get, but if you know of someone who does their own smoking they'll probably find some for you, or you can try looking online. Being Irish, I wouldn't dream of eating smoked fish without wheaten bread. The bread recipe comes from my late grandmother, who was a fantastic baker.

SMOKED FISH PLATTER
with Granny Millar's wheaten bread

for 8–10 as a lunch or starter

12oz (350g) small beets

14oz (400g) small waxy potatoes

10½oz (300g) each of cold-smoked and hot-smoked salmon

5½oz (150g) each of smoked halibut or whitefish, smoked mussels, and smoked prawns (or any combination of your favourite smoked fish)

3½oz (100g) salmon caviar

fronds fresh dill, quarters of lemon

for the watercress sour cream:

1 cup sour cream

3 heaped tbsp mayonnaise

1¾oz (50g) watercress leaves

1½ tsp superfine sugar

1 tsp Dijon mustard

3 good squeezes lemon

for the wheaten bread:

2¼ cups wholewheat flour

½ cup all-purpose flour

1 tsp baking soda

2 tbsp butter

2 tbsp superfine sugar and 1 tsp salt

1 cup buttermilk

1 First make the bread. Preheat the oven to 400°F (200°C). In a bowl, mix the flours and baking soda and rub in the butter. Add the sugar, salt, and buttermilk and mix to a loose dough. Form into a loaf shape and put into a 1lb (500g) bread tin. Sprinkle the top with some oats, if you like, and bake in the preheated oven for 25–30 minutes.

2 To make the watercress sour cream, just put everything in the food processor and pulse mix (you don't want the watercress to be completely puréed).

3 Wrap the beets (unpeeled) loosely in tin foil and put in a small roasting tray. Cook for 1–2 hours at 350°F (180°C), or until tender. Peel them once they are cool enough to handle. Boil or steam the potatoes (unpeeled).

4 Arrange the smoked fish and vegetables on a platter—be careful with the beets as the juices can run, staining everything else—leaving room for a small dish in which to put the salmon caviar. Decorate (with restraint) with dill and lemon. Serve with the watercress dressing, wheaten bread, and butter. You can also provide a bowl of plain sour cream if you'd like something simple as well.

This wonderful autumnal tart, rich and smoky, is good for lunch or dinner. It's good served with a simple watercress or arugula salad. Be sure to use undyed smoked haddock, or substitute with smoked trout or whitefish if you prefer.

SMOKED HADDOCK TART
with spinach and Cheddar

serves 4 as a light main
course, 6 as a starter

for the pastry:

2½ cups all-purpose flour

1 cup (2 sticks) butter

good pinch salt

a little very cold water

for the filling:

9oz (250g) spinach, washed

salt and pepper

12oz (350g) smoked haddock
filet, preferably undyed, skinned

3½oz (100g) mature Cheddar,
grated

1 cup heavy cream

2 medium eggs plus 1 egg yolk

1 For the pastry, put the flour, butter, and salt in a food processor and, using the plastic blade, process the mixture until it resembles breadcrumbs. Add just enough water to make the pastry come together. Wrap in tin foil or plastic wrap and refrigerate for 30 minutes.

2 Preheat the oven to 350°F (180°C). Line a 9-inch (23-cm) tart pan, 1½ inches (4cm) deep, with the pastry and chill for 30 minutes. Prick the bottom of the case with a fork, then fill it with greaseproof paper and baking beans and bake blind in the preheated oven for 12 minutes, removing the paper and beans after 7 minutes.

3 Wilt the spinach in a covered pan using just the water left clinging to it after washing. It should only take about 4 minutes. Drain and, when the spinach is cool enough to handle, squeeze out all the excess water. Chop roughly and season well with salt and pepper.

4 Slice the haddock thinly, making sure that you remove any tiny bones. Put the spinach in the bottom of the tart case and lay the fish on top. Season with salt and pepper (use the salt sparingly) and sprinkle with the cheese. Beat the cream and eggs together lightly, season, and pour into the tart case. Bake in the oven for 45 minutes, or until the tart is set and golden. Let it cool slightly before serving.

"We stepped out into the winter world. It was a world of glass, sparkling and motionless. Vapours had frozen all over the trees and transformed them into confections of sugar. Everything was rigid, locked-up and sealed, and when we breathed the air it smelt like needles and stabbed our nostrils and made us sneeze."

CIDER WITH ROSIE LAURIE LEE

Russians love pies. They joke that a Russian will say: "I couldn't eat another thing but I will have a piece of pie." Their pies are often filled with a plethora of ingredients, with mushrooms and cooked rice being particularly popular.

RUSSIAN SMOKED FISH PIE
with cream cheese pastry

serves 4–6

for the pastry:

½ cup cream cheese

½ cup (1 stick) butter

2 large egg yolks

2 cups all-purpose flour

pinch salt

1½ tsp baking powder

for the filling:

3½oz (100g) long-grain rice

chicken stock or water

salt and pepper

14oz (400g) filet of haddock, cod, or any other white fish

1 cup milk

4½oz (125g) smoked trout, broken into bite-size pieces

4½oz (125g) smoked salmon, roughly chopped

11½oz (325g) mushrooms, cleaned and roughly chopped

⅓ cup (5⅓ tbsp) butter

¼ cup all-purpose flour

juice of ½ lemon

3 tbsp sour cream

3 tbsp finely chopped fresh parsley

1 For the pastry, beat the cream cheese and butter in a mixer, then add 1 of the egg yolks. Stir in the flour, salt, and baking powder, and bring together into a ball. Wrap in plastic wrap and chill for 30 minutes.

2 For the filling, cook the rice in just enough water or chicken stock to cover, until the rice is al dente and the liquid has been absorbed. Season and set aside. Put the white fish in a pan, season, and cover with the milk. Heat until simmering and cook the fish for about 5 minutes. Remove the fish from the milk and put it in a bowl with the other fish. Sauté the mushrooms in 2½ tbsp of the butter until nicely colored and quite dry. Season and add to the fish.

3 Melt the rest of the butter and add the flour to make a roux. Cook over a low heat for a minute, then remove from the heat and gradually add the milk used for cooking the fish. Stir well after each addition of milk until smooth. When you have added all the milk, put the pan back on the heat and bring to the boil, stirring all the time as the sauce thickens. Season and let the sauce simmer for 5 minutes so that the flour gets cooked. Add the lemon juice, sour cream, and parsley, then carefully combine the sauce with the fish and mushrooms.

4 Spread the rice over the bottom of a buttered gratin dish (8 x 10 inches/20 x 26cm and 2½ inches/6cm deep), then pour the sauce on top. Leave it to cool a little. Preheat the oven to 400°F (200°C).

5 Roll out the pastry to fit the dish, wet the edges of the dish, and press it down. Trim off the excess pastry and use to decorate the top. Make a few slits in the center of the pie to let the steam escape, then brush the top with the remaining egg yolk. Bake for 10 minutes, then turn the heat down to 350°F (180°C) and cook for a further 20–25 minutes, until the pastry is golden and cooked.

The flavors of northeast Italy are very distinctive. They love smoky tastes, sturdy ingredients such as polenta and the barleylike grain farro, and eastern exotica such as spices and pomegranates. I had this dish as soon as I arrived in the little Friulian village of Sauris after a terrible drive in thick snow, including an altercation with a snowplow. Elena, the chef-owner of the inn where I was staying, makes this with her own smoked goose, but I've substituted duck as it is easier to buy. This salad was followed by a goulash of beef cheeks, apple strudel, and homemade blackberry grappa—not what you expect in Italy, and more than enough to make me forget about the journey.

SALAD OF SMOKED DUCK
with farro, red chicory, and pomegranates

serves 4

½ onion, finely chopped

½ celery stalk, finely chopped

½ tbsp olive oil

1 tbsp butter

1½oz (45g) farro

3½oz (100g) watercress

1 head red chicory, leaves separated and core discarded

seeds from 1 pomegranate

5½oz (150g) smoked duck breast, cut into neat slices

for the dressing:

small dollop Dijon mustard

salt and pepper

¼ tbsp red wine vinegar

¼ tsp cassis

½ tbsp olive oil

1½ tbsp hazelnut oil

1 Sauté the onion and celery in the olive oil and butter until soft but not colored. Add the farro, stir around in the buttery juices, and just cover with water. Cook until the farro is tender and the liquid has been absorbed (25–35 minutes).

2 To make the dressing put the mustard, salt, pepper, and vinegar in a bowl and whisk in all the other ingredients with a fork. Mix a third of it with the warm farro.

3 In a bowl, combine the watercress, chicory, and pomegranate seeds and add the rest of the dressing. Divide the salad between 4 plates, top with the smoked duck, and put a large spoonful of the dressed farro alongside.

> "*I learnt the names of dogs and ducks and horses, and the smells of seasons—of the scent that drifted across the snow from where the sides of boar were smoked...of the tree that bore three hundred weight in plums...*"
> A LEGACY SYBILLE BEDFORD

This dish, inspired by the flavors of eastern Europe, makes a bit of a change from buckwheat blintzes. I love the rich, buttery taste of smoked eel, but if you're not a fan, smoked salmon will do just as well here. Don't make the relish more than a couple of hours in advance as the apple becomes flaccid. The relish is also excellent with a plate of smoked mackerel. Good as a starter or light lunch.

SMOKED EEL WITH POTATO POPPY SEED CAKES
and apple and beet relish

serves 8

1lb (450g) smoked fillet of eel, skinned

8 heaped tbsp crème fraîche

about ½oz (10–15g) freshly grated horseradish

little sprigs fresh dill or chives

for the relish:

3 smallish fresh beets, about 10½oz (300g) in total

1 eating apple

1 tbsp cider vinegar

¼ red onion

1½ tbsp olive oil

2 tsp light brown sugar

salt and pepper

for the potato cakes:

1lb 8oz (675g) medium potatoes, peeled

1 small onion, finely chopped

2 tbsp olive oil

1½ tbsp poppy seeds

2 tbsp butter, melted

1 To make the relish, preheat the oven to 375°F (190°C). Wrap the beets in tin foil, adding about 3 tbsp of water to it, and place it in a small roasting tray. Roast in the preheated oven until tender (about an hour). Let the beets cool. Turn the oven up to 400°F (200°C).

2 Peel the apple, then core and dice the flesh. Put immediately into a bowl with the vinegar. Slice the onion very fine and sauté it gently for about 1½ minutes in 1 tbsp of the olive oil. You don't want to color or even soften it much, just take the raw edge off it. Add to the bowl with the apples.

3 Peel the cooked beets and cut the flesh into matchsticks. Add to the apples, mix in the sugar and remaining olive oil and season with salt and pepper. Put in the fridge until you need it.

4 For the potato cakes, parboil the potatoes for 10 minutes. Meanwhile, sauté the onion in the olive oil until soft but not colored. Grate the potatoes coarsely and add to the onion. Season well, add the poppy seeds, and mix everything together.

5 Divide the mixture into 8 cakes and put them in a patty tin. Drizzle over the melted butter and cook in the oven for 15 minutes. The cakes should be golden-brown.

6 When they are ready, top with the relish (bring it to room temperature first), then with a small slice of smoked eel, 1 tbsp of crème fraîche, and a sprinkling of horseradish. Decorate each cake with a sprig of dill or a couple of chives.

Yet another dish from Friuli in northeast Italy, where they love smoked flavors. The Friulian village of Sauris is famous for its smoked cured ham, and they also use a lot of smoked ricotta, grated over pumpkin gnocchi and pumpkin-stuffed pasta. Smoked ricotta seems to be impossible to get outside of the area, so this is my reworking of the pasta and pumpkin dish that I ate there.

TAGLIATELLE WITH ROAST PUMPKIN,
sage, ricotta, and smoked cheese

serves 4

3lb 5oz (1.5kg) pumpkin or winter squash

olive oil

⅓ cup (5½ tbsp) butter

salt and pepper

1lb 5oz (600g) fresh tagliatelle

handful sage leaves (about 24)

2oz (50g) ricotta, fresh if possible, forked into chunks

4½oz (125g) smoked cheese, grated

1 Prepare and cook the pumpkin or squash as in the recipe on page 42, drizzling with olive oil and dotting the slices with 1 tbsp of the butter and seasoning.

2 When the squash is almost ready, cook the fresh pasta in boiling water for 4 minutes (or according to the instructions on the pack). Melt the rest of the butter and gently fry the sage leaves in it. When the pasta is ready, drain and stir the butter and sage mixture into it, seasoning well. Gently toss with the roast pumpkin.

3 Divide between plates and top with chunks of ricotta and the grated smoked cheese. Add a good grinding of black pepper.

*"Some weather's coming; you can taste on the sides of
your tongue a quince tang in the air."*

PILGRIM AT TINKER CREEK ANNIE DILLARD

APPLES IN THE ATTIC
apples, pears, and quinces

An apple, the first fruit, is simple and comforting. "A is for Apple" is one of the earliest things we learn. Looking at that cute, bright red fruit on the first page of our ABC, we associate it with safety, comfort, and domesticity. To me, its cheeky shape is endlessly cheering. As early as two years old, I used to swing on the door of the greengrocers demanding "wawos", my baby name for them. But the apple's symbolism is more complicated than a child can comprehend. In religion, mythology, and fairy tales, there is both the good and the bad apple. From Adam and Eve to Snow White, the apple has seduced the innocent. Slice it horizontally and the five seeds form a perfect pentagram, a shape sacred to both Christianity and sorcery, and believed to hold the key to the knowledge of good and evil. Apples are also symbols of immortality and fertility. In England, a girl should put an apple under her pillow on Halloween night if she wants to dream of her husband-to-be; in northern France, the peel of an apple, twirled three times and thrown over the shoulder, is supposed to form the initial of her future spouse. The apple stands for all fruits; it is an emblem of fruitfulness itself.

The American apple grower, Frank Browning, hits the nail on the head when he writes that apples "are as common as toast, as elusive as dreams". We eat more of them than any other fruit, and there are around 8,000 named varieties. But when you see them in the supermarket, reduced to a selection of pallid yellow (Golden Delicious) and bright green (Granny Smith), you understand why most people don't get excited about apples. We are mostly unaware of the diversity of their flavors—nutty, aniseedy, raspberryish—and we purchase them so far from their source that they hold little of the magic of orchards.

If you drive through apple-growing country, whether in New England, Herefordshire, Normandy, or even the Norwegian fjords, it is impossible not to be moved by the apple's varied beauty. Crimson, tawny, ocher, russet, their colors hang heavily on the branch—a perfect metaphor for the bounty of the season—and their sweet odour scents a world otherwise smelling of smoke and decay. The skin can be waxy and slippery, smooth or slightly sandy, but it should always be taut, and then the greatest pleasure is the first bite, when that skin gives way to juice—at once sweet and acidic—and a firm, glassy flesh that breaks with a crunch.

You get to appreciate that there is an apple for every mood and as wide a range of flavors—the product of variety, weather, *terroir,* and grower—as there is in wines. My own preference is for the tarter types. The jolt of acid-drop sourness you get from an Ashmead's Kernel is a wake-up call to the taste buds. It's also worth looking out for the superb sweet-sour Adam's Pearmain, the Allington Pippin that, though almost bitter early in the fall, will taste as honeyed as a quince by Christmas, and the aniseed-flavored Ellison's Orange.

As well as eating apples raw, we cook them into comfortingness. Apples must appear in more comfort-inducing desserts than any other fruit. Tarts, pies, crumbles, cakes, Austrian strudels, Czech *kolaches,* and the American panoply of brown betties, pandowdies, buckles, grunts, and slumps: you can never have too many apple dessert recipes. The apple's sweet acidity, often in conjunction with cider, can create some of the most comforting savory dishes, too. Chicken or pheasant with apples and cream is deeply soothing, and the sight of apples baked around a joint of pork seems to stir something almost primordial in Sunday lunchers. I also like the Scandinavian and Russian habit of adding apple to herring in sour cream and eating it with smoked fish and meat, and the Austrian use of *kren,* an apple and horseradish sauce, to go with *tafelspitz,* their version of *pot-au-feu.*

Compared to the apple, you have to feel sorry for the pear. Whenever I plunder the fruit bowl for a snack to give me a mid-afternoon boost, it will usually be the apple I fall for to put a bounce into my step. The pear, whether long and elegant like the Bose or Conference, or deliciously dumpy like the Comice or William's, looks shy and drowsy in comparison. After all, practically the whole of its body is in its bottom. I won't wake it now, I think. But the pear also has charm. While apples are brisk, pears are sensuous and other-worldly. They can be captured in glass cages in bottles of pear liqueur and have starring roles in nursery rhymes. I can imagine those golden bodies growing alongside silver nutmegs or being delivered with a partridge on the first day of Christmas. The first pear tree that I ever saw, on a misty afternoon in Suffolk, England, was espaliered against the wall of an enclosed garden. It quite took my breath away with its golden beauty and the perfect teardrop shape of its fruit. I imagined that a tree this lovely must have some magic attached to it.

But actually, eating pears frustrates us because they require patience. They are nearly always sold unripe because, fully mature, they are delicate creatures that not only bruise easily, but scar as they bump against sturdier beings. It's not commercially viable to sell them at their peak: you must watch and wait for that time, and their period of optimum loveliness is fleeting. There's an old saying that one must be prepared to sit up at night to eat a ripe pear, its moment of perfection passes so quickly. Keep them at room temperature and don't be tempted to test for ripeness by prodding. Just press the fruit gently near the stem; if it gives a little, it is ready to eat. Test often, or maturity will come and go and you'll have missed the opportunity to bring out their full sweet pearness by eating them with some salty Roquefort or Gorgonzola, or on their own, the juices running down the inside of your sleeve.

There is no pleasure in the grittiness of unripe pear flesh or the mealiness of overripe. But the good news is, it doesn't matter, because a carefully cooked pear is as good as the most perfect ripe one, and there are endless things you can do with them, poaching them in white wine, red wine, cider, Marsala, cassis, or ginger syrup; stuffing them with nuts; or baking them with cranberries. Pears are relatively cheap and, for cooking, ripe ones are too delicate, so those unyielding little bricks are perfect.

Once cooked, apples become fluffy or melting, depending on the variety, while apricots and plums surrender completely. The glory of cooked pears is that the spoon still meets resistance as it slices the flesh, unctuous and satisfying, cutting through the network of softened membranes and fibers. And how that flesh absorbs the flavors around it! That much-derided dish of garnet beauties, pears in red wine, when cooked properly—slowly, then left to sit around in its syrup to intensify both flavor and color—is unrivaled in its capacity to be simple and luscious. If you're lazy, you don't even have to bother peeling pears. Go rustic and lay the halved fruits on their sides in a baking dish, pour over Marsala, add sugar, a couple of sticks of cinnamon, some pats of unsalted butter, and bake slowly in the oven. You'll have a wonderful mellow, warm, wintry dish to serve with cold vanilla ice cream.

The slender brown-and-russet Bosc pear is often recommended for cooking, and it does have firm flesh and keeps its shape well, but I think it can be grainy and has a much less intense flavor the nearer you get to its core. Concorde pears have a vanilla flavor and are great for baking, grilling, or poaching. It may seem sacreligious, but I like cooking with the pears that are also good raw. Bartlett varieties have a quintessential rounded pear shape, a lovely autumnal blush to the skin, and taste distinctly musky. Doyenné du Comice, meaning "top of the show", is the pear par excellence. Not even faintly gritty, it has perfumed, buttery flesh and is so juicy when ripe that you should eat it with a napkin standing by to mop up the stickiness. For a quiet, indulgent, unadulterated pear experience, this is the one to go for.

The quince is exotic and rare, redolent of the spicy East as much as of an English orchard. It is golden, voluptuous, and has an exquisite scent that is reminiscent of honey and tropical fruits. A soft gray down often covers the quince. It is satisfyingly weighty in the hand and opulently sexy piled in a bowl (no wonder it's the fruit of love). While it is not as accessible as the apple or the pear—the flesh is tannic, unyielding and impossible to eat without long, slow cooking—it is rewarding, revealing a rich flavor, very reminiscent of Sauternes, and flesh that cooks to a soft appley-pink or, if baked slowly, a warm, deep amber.

Bake or gently poach quinces with red or white wine and sugar and serve them with cream, or add cooked slices to an apple crumble to increase its scentedness. They are so high in pectin that they make excellent preserves that you can flavor with thyme, sage, or rosemary and use in place of apple jelly. My favorite use for quinces, though, is in savory dishes, particularly pork and game. Put partially cooked halves around a joint of roasting pork, or add slices to a pot-roast pheasant, or make a purée of pears and quinces, spiked with a little ginger, to eat with wild duck. Russians and Georgians cook them, Middle-Eastern style, in spicy meat stews that bring real warmth to autumnal days.

The dishes we cook with these fruits—pears in red wine, stewed apples with cream, pork chops with apple sauce—are gloriously old-fashioned, easy to make, and rooted in the culinary culture of northern Europe and North America. Quinces have long been a marginal fruit, growing in the gardens of aficionados, but the survival of all but the best-known varieties of apple and pear is seriously under threat, as commerce demands long shelf lives and blandness. The best way to honor these lovely fruits is to visit orchards, cider mills, and farmers' markets in search of old and lesser-known varieties, and to let those with the buying power—the supermarkets—know that though apples and pears are as common as toast, we yearn for flavors that are the stuff of dreams.

"Al cafone non far sapere
  Quant'e' buon formaggio e pere"

"Don't let the peasant know
How good are cheese and pears"

ITALIAN FOLK SAYING

I love meals where everything is roasted together and served in the dish in which it has been cooked. The flavors meld, ingredients such as onions become sweet and slightly charred, and there's hardly any dishes to do. You don't need anything more than a few sautéed potatoes and a watercress salad with this. I like sparerib chops—they have such good marbling—but loin chops are fine. Leave out the cheese if you prefer a less rich dish.

ROASTED PORK RIB CHOPS
with pears, onions, and melting Gorgonzola

serves 6

2 red onions

8 slim pears, such as Bosc

6 pork rib chops (about 7oz/200g each)

6 sprigs fresh rosemary

salt and pepper

6 tbsp olive oil

4 tbsp balsamic vinegar

dark brown sugar

6 tbsp mascarpone

5½oz (150g) Gorgonzola or Dolcelatte, cut into big chunks

1 Preheat the oven to 400°F (200°C). Halve the onions and cut into large, half-moon-shaped wedges. Halve and core the pears. Put the chops, onions, pears, and rosemary into a roasting tray, season with salt and pepper, and pour on the olive oil and balsamic vinegar. Turn everything around to make sure it is well seasoned and lightly coated with the oil and vinegar.

2 Roast in the preheated oven for 15 minutes. Turn over the chops, pears, and onions and reduce the heat to 375°F (190°C). Make sure the pears are cut-side-up and sprinkle each one with a little sugar. Roast for another 30 minutes.

3 During the last 15 minutes of cooking time, dot the mascarpone over the top and scatter with the blue cheese. Serve immediately.

A thick bowl of chowder hits the spot for the winter. The New England versions, studded with corn or tomato based, seem better for late summer and early fall eating, but this one, from Quebec, can be downed when there is two feet of snow on the ground.

QUÉBÉCOIS MUSSEL CHOWDER
with cod and cider

serves 4 as a main course

2lb 4oz (1kg) mussels

2½ cups hard cider

2 tbsp butter

2 leeks, cleaned and cut into fine rings

14oz (400g) potatoes, peeled and cut into 1½-inch (4-cm) chunks

½ cup heavy cream

14oz (400g) cod filet (skin removed), cut into 1¼-inch (4-cm) chunks

pepper

squeeze lemon

chopped fresh flat-leaf parsley, to serve

1 Clean the mussels really well, scrubbing the outsides and removing the beards, and discard any that are damaged, open, or do not close when tapped on the side of the sink. Put them into a large saucepan and add the cider. Bring to the boil, turn down to a simmer, cover, and cook for about 5 minutes, or until the mussels have opened. Discard any that remain closed.

2 Melt the butter in a large, heavy-bottomed saucepan and add the leeks and the potatoes. Cover and sweat the vegetables in the butter, plus a splash of water, over a low heat for about 15 minutes, until it starts to soften. Add a little more water every so often to ensure that the vegetables do not burn.

3 When the mussels are cool enough to handle, remove them from the cider and take the meat out of most of them, keeping some in the shell; they look nice in the final dish. Add the cider and mussel juices to the leek, and potatoes and simmer until the potatoes are tender. Gently mash some of the potatoes to slightly thicken the juices. Add the cream and cod and, over a gentle heat, poach the cod for 2–3 minutes. Add the mussels to the soup and heat through. Season with pepper and a good squeeze of lemon (you shouldn't need any salt as mussel liquor is usually pretty salty). Scatter with the parsley and serve.

"Of the crow-blue mussel-shells, one keeps
adjusting the ash-heaps;
opening and shutting itself like an injured fan."
THE FISH MARIANNE MOORE

There's something very satisfying about pot roasting. That hit of cooking aromas, heat, and moisture as you lift the lid is very comforting. You'd be as likely to find this dish—based on the classic English West Country ingredients of cider and apples—in Normandy as you would in England.

WEST COUNTRY POT ROAST CHICKEN
with apples and cider

serves 6–8

2 tbsp butter

3½–4lb (1.75kg) chicken

7oz (200g) bacon in one piece, cut into chunks about ¾ inch (2cm) square

2 onions, cut in half-moon slices

1 cup hard cider

salt and pepper

4 sprigs fresh rosemary

3 dessert apples, peeled, cored, and cut into wedges

a little granulated sugar

⅔ cup heavy cream

2½ tsp Dijon mustard

1 Preheat the oven to 325°F (170°C).

2 Melt half the butter in a large, heavy-bottomed casserole dish into which the chicken will fit quite snugly. Season the chicken and brown it gently on all sides. I use a couple of big wooden spoons to move it around so I don't pierce the skin.

3 Carefully remove the chicken from the dish and set it aside. In the same dish, cook the bacon until golden on all sides, then add the onions and cook for a few minutes more, just to get them nice and buttery.

4 Put the chicken back in the dish on top of the bacon and onions and add the cider. Bring to the boil and immediately turn down to a very gentle simmer. Season with salt and pepper, add the rosemary, and cover the dish.

5 Cook in the preheated oven for 1½ hours. When it is cooked, the juices between the leg and the main body of the chicken should run clear when pierced at the thickest part.

6 While waiting for the bird to finish cooking, quickly sauté the apples in the remaining butter until just tender, sprinkling them with a little sugar to give sweetness and help them color.

7 When the chicken is cooked, carefully remove it from the dish, cover with tin foil, and keep warm in a low oven. Bring the juices in the dish to the boil and add the cream and mustard. Boil until you have a sauce that will just coat the back of a spoon. Check the seasoning and add the cooked apples. Serve the chicken, either whole or jointed, with the sauce.

This dish from the Savoie region of France looks lovely—it comes out of the oven a beautiful burnished gold—and is utterly simple.

POIRES SAVOYARDS

serves 4–6

4 large pears, such as Bosc

pat unsalted butter

4 tbsp superfine sugar

¾ cup heavy cream

splash vanilla extract

1 Preheat the oven to 400°F (200°C). Peel the pears, halve them, remove the cores, and slice lengthways into pieces about ¼ inch (5mm) thick at the thickest part.

2 Butter a shallow ovenproof dish and arrange the pears in it, overlapping. Sprinkle on the sugar. Mix the cream with a drop of vanilla extract and pour over the pears. Bake for 20 minutes. Let it cool slightly and serve.

We don't really cook dinner dishes as old-fashioned as this any more, but *hete bliksem*, as its known in its native Holland, is delicious on a cold winter evening. And who can resist such a name?

HOT LIGHTNING

serves 4

2lb 4oz (1kg) small new potatoes, scrubbed

9oz (250g) tart eating apples, such as Granny Smith

9oz (250g) pears

¼ cup (½ stick) butter

14oz (400g) bacon, cut into chunks about ¾ inch (2cm) square

salt and pepper

light brown sugar

leaves from 2 sprigs fresh thyme

1 Halve the potatoes or cut them into chunks about 1¼ inches (3cm) square. Core and quarter the apples and pears and cut into slices lengthways; they should be about ¼ inch (5mm) thick at the thickest part. Melt the butter in a heavy-bottomed casserole dish and sauté the bacon and potatoes until golden all over. Add the fruit and turn it over in the buttery juices. Season and add sugar and thyme to taste.

2 Cover the casserole dish with a lid and cook over a very low heat on top of the stove, or in an oven preheated to 325°F (170°C), for 30 minutes or so, or until everything is tender. You need to shake the dish every so often to prevent everything from sticking. Add a splash of water to the mixture if it is becoming too dry.

3 Check the seasoning and serve just as it is (wilted Savoy cabbage is delicious with it), or with sausages or pork chops.

Friuli, in northeast Italy, has a unique cuisine. The flavors of the Austro-Hungarian empire, Slovenia, and Venice all come together here, and perhaps because snow has always kept it rather cut off geographically, it has retained many old-fashioned dishes and its own culinary identity. Spices are used more here than in any other region of Italy. They love fruit, too—especially apples—and there are recipes galore for apple tarts, such as this one. You may need to go to a specialist wine store to find grappa, but it's well worth it.

FRIULIAN APPLE, WALNUT,
and poppy seed tart

serves 8

2½ cups all-purpose flour

½ cup (1 stick) butter

½ cup superfine sugar

1 tsp baking powder

grated zest of ½ lemon

1 tbsp grappa

2 tbsp cold whole milk

for the filling:

3 tart eating apples

6oz (175g) shelled walnuts

1½ tbsp grappa

grated zest of ½ lemon

2¼oz (60g) raisins

3 tbsp poppy seeds

½ tsp ground cinnamon

½ tsp ground ginger

ground seeds of 5 cardamom pods

to finish:

confectioners sugar and 1½ tbsp poppy seeds

whipped cream and grappa

1 Put the flour and butter in a food processor with a plastic blade attached and process until the mixture resembles breadcrumbs. Add the superfine sugar, baking powder, and lemon zest and mix again, adding first the grappa and then the milk, until the pastry comes together in a ball (you may not need to use all the milk). Wrap in plastic wrap and chill for at least 30 minutes. Preheat the oven to 375°F (190°C) and put a metal baking tray inside.

2 Divide the dough into 2 pieces, one two thirds of the dough and the other one third. On a floured surface, roll out the larger piece and use it to line a greased 9-inch (22-cm) springform cake tin. You want to line the bottom and have the pastry form sides, 1½ inches (4cm) high, all the way around. Chill. Roll the other piece of pastry into a circle just slightly larger than the cake tin. Put that on a floured metal tray and let that chill too.

3 To make the filling, peel and grate the apples, chop the walnuts and mix both with all the other ingredients. Pile this into the lined cake tin and place the other circle of pastry on top. Pinch the edges of the pastry together and then crimp them. Cut a little star, to let the steam out, in the middle of the pastry top. Put on the baking tray in the preheated oven and cook for 30 minutes.

4 Let the tart cool in the tin, then carefully remove it. Sift confectioners sugar over the top and scatter with poppy seeds. Serve with whipped cream after adding another slosh of grappa.

With all the flavor of an apple pie—but less hassle to make—these should come with a health warning: they are seriously addictive. It's best to eat them the day they are made, which shouldn't be too taxing.

SOUR CREAM APPLE-PIE MUFFINS
with pecans and brown sugar

makes 14–16

for the filling and topping:

4½oz (125g) shelled pecans, chopped (but still coarse)

½ cup light brown sugar

½ tsp ground cinnamon

for the batter:

4 cups all-purpose flour, sifted

2 tsp baking powder

½ cup (1 stick) butter, softened, plus a little extra for greasing

¼ cup light brown sugar

pinch salt

½ tsp cinnamon

9oz (250g) chopped cooking apple, peeled

1 cup sour cream

2 tbsp whole milk

1 egg, beaten

I Preheat the oven to 350°F (180°C). Mix together the nuts, sugar, and cinnamon for the filling and topping. Set aside. Put the flour and baking powder in a large bowl and rub in the butter. Stir in the sugar, salt, cinnamon, and apple flesh. Mix the sour cream with the milk and egg and gradually add that to the bowl as well. Don't overwork the mixture, just stir well to combine.

2 Spoon a layer of the mixture into each hole in buttered muffin tins, then sprinkle half the nut-and-sugar filling on top. Spoon the rest of the batter onto each muffin and sprinkle the rest of the nut-and-sugar mixture over them. Bake for 20 minutes, or until a skewer inserted into the center of a muffin comes out clean. Leave to rest in the tin for 5 minutes, then turn them out. Cool on a wire cooling rack.

"My long two-pointed ladder's sticking through a tree
Towards heaven still,
And there's a barrel that I didn't fill
Beside it, and there may be two or three
Apples I didn't pick upon some bough.
But I am done with apple-picking now."

AFTER APPLE-PICKING ROBERT FROST

We rarely eat desserts as substantial as this nowadays, but on one of those Sunday afternoons when the light seems to fade at about 3 o'clock, there is nothing like a steamed dessert to cheer you up. Golden syrup is popular in Great Britain and can sometimes be found in speciality stores. If you can't get hold of any, combine 1½ tbsp of light corn syrup with ½ tbsp of molasses.

STEAMED APPLE AND MARMALADE DESSERT

serves 6

¾ cup superfine sugar

¾ cup (1½ sticks) butter, plus a little extra for greasing

3 eggs, beaten

¾ cup self-rising flour, sifted

2 cooking apples, peeled, and flesh chopped into chunks ¾ inch (2cm) square

pinch salt

1oz (30g) soft white breadcrumbs

whole milk

6 tbsp orange marmalade

2 tbsp golden syrup

I Cream the sugar and butter together until fluffy. Gradually add the eggs, beating well. Using a large spoon, fold in the flour and apples, then the salt and breadcrumbs. Add enough milk to make a dropping consistency.

2 Put the marmalade and syrup into the bottom of a buttered dessert bowl (it will help if it has a rim). Pour in the cake mixture. Cover with buttered tin foil, pleated in the middle to allow for expansion, and secure this by tying it with string round the rim of the bowl. Make a secure handle by threading more string through the string tied around the rim.

3 Put the bowl on top of a trivet in a large saucepan and pour in boiling water. (The tin foil shouldn't touch the water or you'll end up with a soggy cake). You can also cook the cake in a large steamer. Cover the saucepan and steam for 1½ hours, until firm and well risen, topping up with boiling water when needed. Remove from the heat and leave to shrink a little before turning out on to a warmed plate.

"...this country bedroom, raw
 With the touch of dawn, wrapped in a minor peace,
 Hears through an open window the garden draw
 Long pitch black breaths, lay bare its apple trees,
 Ripe pear trees, brambles, windfall-sweetened soil..."

ANOTHER SEPTEMBER **THOMAS KINSELLA**

"As it is, in my view, the duty of an apple to be crisp and crunchable, a pear should have such a texture as leads to silent consumption"

ANATOMY OF DESSERT EDWARD BUNYARD

The name of this old-fashioned dessert, which both Norway and Denmark lay claim to, always makes me think of Scandinavian children out gathering apples in their aprons. It's also known as "Veiled Farm Girls", and "Peasant Girls in a Veil"; I suppose the veil and mist both refer to the blanket of cream.

PEASANT GIRLS IN A MIST

serves 4–6

2 large cooking apples

3 tbsp superfine sugar

2 tbsp unsalted butter

3½oz (100g) wheat and rye bread, pulsed into breadcrumbs

¼ cup light brown sugar

½ tsp ground cinnamon

1¼ cup heavy cream

4 tbsp confectioners sugar

really good squeeze lemon

1½ tbsp toasted hazelnuts, very roughly chopped

1 Peel and core the apples and cut them into chunks. Put them in a saucepan with the superfine sugar and 2 tbsp water and cook over a gentle heat until they are completely tender. Stir every so often and mash the fruit down roughly with the back of a wooden spoon. Check for sweetness—I prefer it not too sweet as it is being mixed with sweet cream and breadcrumbs—and put it into a bowl to cool.

2 Melt the butter in a frying pan and add the breadcrumbs and the brown sugar. Sauté, stirring constantly, over a medium heat until the breadcrumbs are golden. Add the cinnamon and continue to cook for about a minute. Leave to cool.

3 Whip the cream, adding the confectioners sugar and squeeze of lemon (add the lemon before the cream is too thick as the acid in the lemon has a thickening effect), then layer the stewed apples, breadcrumbs, and whipped cream mixtire in a glass bowl, ending with a layer of cream. Scatter with the chopped hazelnuts.

I first tasted apple bread in a little restaurant in Normandy and never saw it again until I discovered it in one of my favorite British pubs, the Dartmoor Inn at Lydford in Devon. It's incredible with cheese, pork terrines, and pâtés.

THE DARTMOOR INN'S APPLE BREAD

makes 4 loaves

2 cooking apples, peeled, cored, and sliced

1 cup water

3 eating apples, peeled, cored, and diced into ½ inch (1cm) squares

½ cup butter

4 cups wholewheat flour

2 cups bread flour

3 tsp salt

15g dried yeast

¼ cup superfine sugar

1 egg yolk, lightly beaten, for glazing

1 Put the cooking apples in a pan with half the water and simmer to a purée. Fry the eating apples lightly in 2 tbsp of the butter until golden brown in color.

2 In a large bowl place all the brown and white flour and salt. Melt the remaining butter and set to one side to cool slightly. Heat the remaining water until tepid. Add the yeast and 2 tsp sugar and leave somewhere warm for 15 minutes. Mix the rest of the sugar with the flours. Make a well in the centre and add the melted butter and the yeast mixture. Now add the slightly warm cooking apple purée and the fried eating apples. Stir with a wooden spoon, then bring together with your hands into a dough. If the dough seems too dry and will not hold together, add a little water. If it seems too wet, add a little more flour.

3 Place the dough on a lightly floured work surface and knead for 10–15 minutes, until smooth. Put in a clean bowl, cover with lightly oiled plastic wrap and place in a warm area until doubled in size (this will take about 45 minutes).

4 Knead again for about a minute, then divide it into 4 pieces, shape into loaves, and place on a lightly oiled baking tray. Allow to proof for about 30 minutes in a warm place, then glaze the loaves with the egg yolk. Preheat the oven to 350°F (180°C).

5 Bake for 35 minutes. Remove the loaves and tap them on the bottom to ensure that they sound hollow. If not, put them back in the oven for a few more minutes. Place the loaves on a wire cooling rack.

"Honey-white figs of the north,
black figs with scarlet inside, of the south.
Ripe figs won't keep, won't keep in any clime."

FIGS D.H. LAWRENCE

THE COLOR PURPLE
plums, damsons, and figs

For a bit of dark, seductive glamour in the cold months, I turn to plums, figs, and sour little black damsons. The misty bloom of their skins, the spectrum of colors they encompass—purple, black, dark blue, amber, and russet—and the texture of those skins, somewhere between velvet and suede, echo the softer fabrics we begin to wear once September arrives. I'm drawn to their rich, purplish blotches of color: study them through half-closed eyes, and it looks as though they've been drawn in smudgy, pastels.

Of course, plums and figs are summer as well as fall fruits—you see the first of them in July. But classic summer fruits, such as tart, bright raspberries, and strawberries, put a spring in your step and make you think of blue skies; plums and figs make me want to close the front door and put the oven on. I'm a sucker for baked and poached fruits, and plums and figs take to this treatment perfectly. Poach or bake them in red wine with sugar or honey, and with herbs such as thyme, fennel, bay leaves, and rosemary, or spices such as cinnamon, ginger, and cardamom—each combination will give different results. Scoop the fruits out of the cooking liquid when they are just tender, reduce the juice, pour it over the fruit, and chill: simple and delicious.

Figs are the product of warm climates and bring with them the flavor of the Middle East; but they are also as much part of fall and winter eating in cool countries as cinnamon and cloves. As a Brit, I have long loved the dried version in rich fruit dessert (and those ghastly oversweet cookies, fig rolls). When I was a child, my mother used to buy blocks of dried figs, the sides mottled with seeds that looked like squashed insects, from which we cut slivers for snacks. It wasn't the best introduction to the fruit, but now that dried figs are lusciously moist, they are losing their "healthy-and-good-for-you" image. I always have a couple of bags in the cupboard and pounce on the fresh ones as soon as they appear.

The cooking of southwest France supplies plenty of ideas about what to do with figs in the darker months. The summers in this region are warm enough to allow the fruit to grow, but it is so cold in the fall that the character of this essentially Mediterranean fruit completely changes as it is served with rich confit of duck and salads of smoked meat, braised with guinea fowl and chestnuts, or eaten raw with Roquefort and walnuts. Figs work just as well in savory dishes as they do in sweet ones and can be cooked in a similar way for both. Sprinkle halved fresh figs with brown sugar and maybe a little booze and grill for 4 minutes until caramelized, then serve them with grilled duck breasts, slices of Parma ham, and walnuts, or chunks of blue cheese, or else with honey-drizzled mascarpone and shortbread for a simple dessert. If you don't want to cook them—preferring not to tamper with that bloomy skin and sensual shape—offer whole raw figs at the end of a meal with a chalky goat's milk cheese, or in a bowl along with some ripe purple plums.

Plums—soft, small and gentle on your lips—are my favorite fruit to snack on and one of the most useful in the autumnal kitchen. The Austrians put them into tarts, pastry slices, cakes, and dumplings, and the Hungarians, Poles, and Russians can't get enough of them, either, making them into plum brandy and vodka, or using them in sauces to eat with game, grilled chicken, and lamb kebabs. Plums can be a lottery, however. They often look as if they'll be full of sweet-sour purple juice, but taste of nothing. Luckily, even a poor plum responds well to heat and sugar, so it's poaching or roasting for them. Victorias, the plums we see most of, are the Golden Delicious of the plum world: bland, without the requisite touch of sharpness that makes a really good plum. But I still use them, enhanced with lemon juice, when they are cheap and abundant. Better are the more marginal varieties of plum, such as Warwickshire Drooper, Kirkes Blue, and Purple Pershore. Farmers' markets and farm shops are the places to look for such fruit. Gages are generally considered to have the best flavor of all. The greengage, or *Reine Claude* as it is known in France, is available from late August and is perfect for French-style open tarts or just eating out of your hand. Gages are sweeter and more delicate than most plums, and you shouldn't miss the chance to eat a Coe's Golden Drop, of which the epicure Edmund Bunyard wrote, in *The Anatomy of Dessert:* "…the skin is rather tough, but between this and the stone floats an ineffable nectar." I'm very influenced by color, though; I want bloodred juices staining my crumbles, so it's the dark ones I will always choose for cooking.

Damsons, those small, dark oval plums, are the most tart, most intensely flavored of all autumnal fruits. Their deep crimson color is so spectacular, it's no wonder they were used as a dye in the past. Don't think about eating them raw: they need both sugar and cooking to get the best out of them. And forget about trying to remove the pits. The pit is so tightly embedded that it won't budge. For jam and chutney—and damsons are great for these, producing big, dark, fruity jarfuls—remove the stones after cooking using a sieve. Another good way to use damsons is in crumbles, pies, and cobblers: their sourness really cuts through pastry. For these, I leave it to diners to pick out the pits.

You have to be quick to get hold of damsons, though, and it's best to know someone with a tree. They're picked from the end of August for about 8 weeks, and supermarkets and grocery stores largely seem to ignore them, but then there is something special about a fruit that takes effort to track down. It seems appropriate to make old-fashioned country dishes with them. Damson cheese, a dark firm jelly made from boiling and reducing damson flesh with sugar, is a better foil for lamb than redcurrant jelly and superb with strong cheeses. The deep, fruity flavor will keep you going through the winter months.

Sadly, prunes still suffer from being the subject of schoolboy giggles because of their laxative qualities. It's an ingredient I hesitate to cook for people I don't know well in case they associate prunes with dormitory rooms, navy blazers, and Latin conjugations, but other Europeans love them. Again, it's the cooks of southwest France, where the fruit was traditionally shipped through the port of Agen (hence the name for their prunes, *pruneaux d'Agen*), who can teach us how to use them: rabbit, pork, and duck legs are braised with prunes, spiced prunes are served with pork and rabbit terrines, and their dessert table boasts prune *clafoutis*, prune tart, and prune-and-Armagnac ice cream. Why don't we honor this dark fruit in such a way? The Danes love them, too, stuffed into loin of pork or pickled and eaten with open sandwiches, and the Russians and the Poles both eat them in pork dishes and in festive compotes, poached along with dried figs.

I'm not convinced that the best prunes are from Agen, despite their reputation. There are very good Californian ones, and I select them according to how I want to cook them. *Mi-cuit*, the semi-dried ones, don't have the shelf life of the fully dried ones but are delicious for snacks, make great "devils-on-horseback", and are good in any dish in which they won't be cooked for long. For compotes or pickling, I buy the properly dried ones, which need to be soaked. The ones to be careful of, delicious though they may be, are those in between fully dried and *mi-cuit*: they can catch you unawares by falling apart completely when cooked. You want your prunes to have a bit of body.

The prune's flavor bears little relation to that of the plum. The fresh plum is tart and fresh, while the dried version is sweet and chocolatey, and will immediately bring a richness to your taste buds. Apart from pairing them with rabbit—my favorite combination—prunes are excellent standbys for making easy desserts. They keep for ages in their sealed packages, ready to be whipped out in an emergency and poached in wine or black tea and sugar, soaked in cognac or Armagnac and eaten with ice cream, or stuffed, Russian-style, with a walnut before being doused in whipped cream. Stephanie Alexander, in her beautiful book *Travelling and Eating in South-West France*, writes about prunes she was offered in place of dessert. They had been pitted, stuffed with marzipan and half a walnut, dipped in dark chocolate, and, once set, individually wrapped in deep-blue tissue paper. With a bitter espresso, I can't think of a more delicious end to a wintry meal.

"I have eaten
    the plums
    that were in
    the icebox

    and which
    you were probably
    saving
    for breakfast

    Forgive me
    they were delicious
    so sweet
    and so cold"

THIS IS JUST TO SAY WILLIAM CARLOS WILLIAMS

Russians absolutely love Georgian food. It's partially that they are seduced by the Georgians themselves—dark-eyed, romantic, fiery—but they are also enchanted by their use of exotic spices and their unusual combination of herbs (in Georgian cooking you will find dill, basil, and cilantro all rubbing shoulders in the same dish). So while this dish has echoes of both Persian and Indian cooking, you will find it being eaten in the snows of Russia.

GEORGIAN LAMB
with damsons and walnuts

serves 4

3 tbsp peanut oil

1lb 10oz (750g) boneless lamb stew meat, cut into chunks 1¼ inch (3cm) square

2 onions, roughly chopped

4 garlic cloves, finely chopped

½ tsp ground coriander seeds

¼ tsp turmeric

½ tsp crushed fenugreek

¾ tsp cayenne pepper

1½ tbsp all-purpose flour

water or lamb or light chicken stock

salt and pepper

good pinch saffron threads, steeped in 3 tbsp boiled water

2 bay leaves

leaves from 2 sprigs fresh thyme

4oz (115g) shelled walnuts, roughly crushed in a mortar and pestle

20 fresh damsons (or plums)

2 tbsp light brown sugar

2 tbsp pomegranate molasses

2 tbsp each fresh cilantro and flat-leaf parsley, roughly chopped, to serve

1 Heat 2 tbsp of the oil in a heavy-bottomed casserole dish and sauté the lamb on all sides until brown. Do this in batches so that the pan doesn't become overcrowded, or the lamb will sweat and not color. Spoon the lamb out and set it aside. Add the rest of the oil and sauté the onions until soft and just beginning to color. Add the garlic and cook for a further minute.

2 Put the lamb back into the dish and add the ground coriander seeds, turmeric, fenugreek, and cayenne pepper. Stir everything around for a minute to give the spices a chance to release their aromas. Add the flour, mix well, and let this cook for another minute. Add the water or stock—just enough to cover the meat—and the rest of the ingredients, apart from the fresh cilantro and parsley. If you are using plums, you can halve and pit them; for damsons, just leave them intact. Season well with salt and pepper and bring to the boil. Immediately turn the heat down, cover the casserole dish and simmer over a very low heat for 1½–2 hours, or cook in the oven at 275°F (140°C). The meat should be completely tender. Check the level of the liquid every so often. It shouldn't get too dry, but you want enough to evaporate so that the stew is quite thick. If it seems too soupy, remove the lid 15 minutes before the end of cooking time.

3 Stir in the fresh cilantro and parsley, check the seasoning, and serve. Remind your diners to remove the pits as they eat.

The Danes, hands down, do the best northern Christmas meal. It is eaten on Christmas Eve and is always based on goose or duck accompanied by fruit, often apples or prunes. This dish, which combines northern rye bread with succulent southern figs, makes a glamorous version of the Danish Christmas feast, and one that you could eat for any celebratory meal in the fall and winter. You can use the same stuffing for duck. Braised red cabbage is a must on the side.

ROAST GOOSE
with brandied fig, chestnut, and rye stuffing

serves 8

13lb (6kg) goose, giblets removed

salt and pepper

2 tbsp honey (optional)

2 eating apples (optional)

for the stuffing:

9½oz (275g) dried figs (the moist, no-need-to-soak type)

½ cup Calvados or brandy

3 onions, finely chopped

5 celery stalks, plus leaves, finely chopped

⅓ cup (5⅓ tbsp) butter

9½oz (275g) rye bread, pulsed into breadcrumbs

14oz (400g) cooked chestnuts (vacuum-packed is fine)

4½oz (125g) fresh cranberries, very roughly chopped

3 garlic cloves, crushed

I Preheat the oven to 400°F (200°C). Pull away all the excess lumps of fat from inside the goose. Wash the bird inside and out and pat dry. Prick the breast of the goose, neck area, and back—this helps the fat drain off—but don't push the fork through to the flesh. Season well, inside and out, with salt and pepper.

2 For the stuffing, put the dried figs into a saucepan with the Calvados or brandy and bring to the boil. Gently simmer for 15 minutes, then let the figs sit in the liquid.

3 In a saucepan, sauté the onion and celery in the butter until soft but not colored. Put in a large bowl. Chop the figs and add to the bowl, with their soaking liquid, along with all the other stuffing ingredients. Mix well and taste to check for seasoning.

4 Stuff the goose. I always put an apple or two into the cavity as well as at the end—they're a delicious extra that someone always wants, and they keep the stuffing in—but they're optional. Put the goose onto a wire rack in a roasting tray. Roast in the preheated oven for 30 minutes, then turn the heat down to 350°F (180°C) and roast for another 3 hours. Drain off the fat from time to time—keep it for the roasted potatoes. You hardly need me to remind you to be careful when removing the fat: it is hot!

2 small eggs, beaten

1½ tsp juniper berries, crushed

leaves from 5 sprigs fresh thyme

for the gravy:

4 shallots, chopped

1 small carrot, diced

1 celery stalk, diced

2 tbsp butter

¼ cup Calvados

3½ cups goose stock, made from the wing tips and giblets, or really well-flavored chicken stock

beurre manié (optional):

¾ tbsp all-purpose flour

¾ tbsp softened butter

5 If you want the goose to look glossy, spread it with the honey before the last 15 minutes of cooking time. Leave this step out if you think this will make it too sweet, but I do it. When the goose is cooked, take it out of the oven and put onto a heated platter. Cover it with tin foil and let it rest for 15–20 minutes.

6 To make the gravy, sauté the shallots, carrot, and celery in the butter until golden-brown all over. Pour on the Calvados and reduce until only a couple of tablespoons remain. Add the stock, bring to the boil, and leave to simmer for half an hour. Strain through a sieve. Now boil to reduce the liquid, or, if you already think the flavor is intense enough but you want it to be thicker, mash the butter and flour together to make a *beurre manié*, and whisk it into the gravy.

7 Serve the goose on a platter. Grilled or roast fresh figs and small baked apples look beautiful around it.

We do so much long, slow cooking in fall and winter that it's good to have a few quick-cook dishes in your repertoire using seasonal ingredients. This dish is very last-minute, so make sure your accompaniments are simple or can be prepared in advance. I like it with sautéed potatoes and a watercress salad.

HONEYED DUCK BREASTS
with figs, chestnuts, and shallots

serves 4

4 duck breast filets

2 tbsp dark brown sugar

½ tsp ground cinnamon

2 tbsp balsamic vinegar

4 tbsp hard cider

salt and pepper

8 shallots

5 tbsp honey

4 fresh figs, halved

12 cooked chestnuts

1 tbsp olive oil

1 Make 3 slashes in the skin of each duck breast with a small, sharp knife. Mix the sugar, cinnamon, 1 tbsp of the balsamic vinegar, cider, salt, and pepper in a small dish and put the duck breasts into this, turning them over to make sure they get coated in the marinade. Cover loosely, put in the fridge, and leave to marinate for several hours, turning the breasts over every so often.

2 Put the peeled shallots in a small saucepan and cover with water. Bring to the boil and simmer until tender. Drain and set aside.

3 Preheat the oven to 400°F (200°C). Heat a griddle pan. Dry the skin of the duck breasts and put them onto the griddle pan, skin-side-down, over a medium-to-high heat. Cook the duck for about 4 minutes, until the skin is brown but not burned; it will cook in the fat that runs from underneath the skin. Paint the duck breasts all over with about 2 tbsp of the honey, season all over with salt and pepper, and put them, skin-side-up, in a small roasting tray. Spoon over the remaining marinade and cook in the oven for 7 minutes.

4 While the duck is cooking, drain the duck fat off the griddle. Put the figs, chestnuts, and shallots in a small bowl with the rest of the balsamic vinegar and honey, olive oil, and a seasoning of salt and pepper. Heat the griddle and put the figs on it. Cook quickly on both sides, just long enough to allow the figs to soften and char slightly. Add the chestnuts and shallots and cook for long enough for the figs to heat through and become caramelized in the honey.

5 Let the duck breasts rest for 3 minutes, covered, and kept warm, then cut them into neat slices across the breast and serve immediately with the figs, chestnuts, and shallots.

You can use vacuum-packed, ready-cooked chestnuts for this, or see the chapter on chestnuts (page 28) for how to cook your own. Try replacing the figs with field mushrooms (in which case, leave out the sugar) if you want something more meaty and savory. Both make great vegetarian main courses.

ROAST FIGS, SHALLOTS, AND CHESTNUTS
with Gorgonzola polenta

serves 8

10¾ cups vegetable stock

1lb (450g) coarse cornmeal (polenta)

salt and pepper

1lb 12oz (800g) shallots, peeled

6 tbsp olive oil

3 tbsp balsamic vinegar

4 sprigs fresh rosemary

18 figs

pinch light brown sugar

13oz (375g) cooked chestnuts (shelled weight)

¼ cup (½ stick) butter

5oz (140g) Parmesan, grated

14oz (400g) Gorgonzola, cut into ¾-inch (2-cm) chunks

1 Put the stock in a heavy-bottomed saucepan and bring to the boil. Pour the polenta into the stock in a steady stream, stirring all the time. Lumps may start to form, but beat hard and they will break down. Turn the heat down, season well with salt and pepper, and keep stirring until the polenta is cooked—about 45 minutes. (If you're using quick-cook polenta, it should be done in 5–10 minutes.) The polenta is ready when it comes away from the sides of the pan.

2 While the polenta is cooking, preheat the oven to 375°F (190°C). Put the shallots in a roasting tray big enough to hold the figs and chestnuts as well. Pour a little of the olive oil and some of the balsamic vinegar over the shallots, season with salt and pepper, add the rosemary sprigs, and put in the preheated oven for 20 minutes.

3 Quarter the figs without cutting right through, so that each one opens up like a flower. Add to the shallots, spoon over the rest of the olive oil and balsamic vinegar, season with salt and pepper, stir, and sprinkle a little brown sugar over each fig. Add the chestnuts, spooning the cooking juices over them. Cook for a further 5 minutes. (You do not cook them right through; they will continue to cook on top of the polenta.)

4 When the polenta is cooked, add the butter and Parmesan and check the seasoning. Grease a broad, shallow ovenproof dish and pour half the polenta into it. Dot with one third of the cut-up Gorgonzola, then pour on the rest of the polenta. Top with the figs, shallots and chestnuts and dot with the rest of the Gorgonzola. Pour any cooking juices over the top. Bake in the oven for 15 minutes, then grill very quickly under a high heat to brown the melted cheese.

Figs, of course, come from the Mediterranean, but like exotic spices such as ginger and cinnamon, we see them as a prime autumnal ingredient in northern kitchens. The appearance of their bloomy purple bodies is as much a sign that fall has arrived as are squash and wild mushrooms. I like this dessert chilled, but you can serve it warm or at room temperature if you prefer. Replace the vodka with extra red wine if you feel this is a little too boozy. The blackberries look gorgeous—like glistening, antique buttons—but if you can't get them, use small seedless black grapes instead. Serve with ginger cookies, either bought, or the Scandinavian *pepparkakor* on page 162.

ROAST FIGS AND PLUMS IN VODKA
with cardamom cream

serves 8

16 fresh firm figs

12 firm plums

⅔ cup red wine

½ cup vodka, plus a little extra

¾ cup granulated sugar

6 tbsp cassis, plus a little extra

10½oz (300g) blackberries (if available) or seedless black grapes

to serve:

4 cardamom pods

1⅓ cups heavy cream

confectioners sugar

1 Preheat the oven to 350°F (180°C). Cut the figs in half, lengthways, without slicing all the way through. Halve the plums and remove the pits. Put the figs and plums into a shallow ovenproof dish that will hold the fruit in a single layer.

2 Mix the wine, vodka, ½ cup of the granulated sugar and 4 tbsp of the cassis in a pan and heat, stirring to help the sugar dissolve. Simmer until reduced by one third, then pour it over the fruit. Sprinkle the rest of the sugar on top of the fruit.

3 Bake in the preheated oven for 25–30 minutes. (If you are using grapes instead of blackberries, add the grapes 15 minutes before the end of cooking time.) The fruit should be soft, but not collapsing, and slightly caramelized on top. Let the fruit cool, then add the blackberries, if using. Pour a shot of vodka over the fruit and drizzle with a couple more tablespoons of cassis.

4 Remove the seeds from the cardamom pods and grind them in a mortar and pestle, or in a heavy bowl using the end of a rolling pin.

5 Put the cream in a bowl, add the crushed cardamom, and whip the cream, adding confectioners sugar to taste. Serve with the fruit.

Some of the best English dishes are completely neglected nowadays. Fruit cheese, a firm, jellylike fruit purée that you slice and eat with savory food—strong cheeses, lamb, and game—or just as a sweetmeat, is a great old-fashioned English tracklement (relish) and very easy to make. It's like the Spanish *membrillo* (which you're more likely to have eaten, since you can sometimes find it in delis), but made from damsons instead of quinces. You can also make it with plums when damsons aren't in season. A moist, garnet-colored slab of this damson cheese is just wonderful with many cheeses.

DAMSON CHEESE

4lb 8oz (2kg) damsons (or plums)

granulated sugar

I Put the damsons in a big, heavy-bottomed pan with about 4 tbsp of water. Simmer gently until the damsons are soft and tender, turning and squashing them with a wooden spoon every so often. Sieve the cooked damsons to remove the skin and pits, pressing really firmly to get as much purée as possible. Measure the purée and add 1½ cups sugar for every 1 pint (2½ cups).

2 Put the purée and sugar back into the heavy pan and simmer over a low heat, stirring to help the sugar dissolve. Cook, stirring regularly to make sure that the purée doesn't catch on the bottom of the pan, until you have a thick, grainy paste. It is ready when the spoon, dragged across the bottom, leaves a clear channel in the fruit purée—this can take as long as an hour.

3 Pour the purée into shallow plastic containers and leave to cool. It seems to keep almost indefinitely in the fridge.

Traditional British Christmas pudding is so easy—the most taxing part is getting the ingredients out of the cupboard—that I don't know why more people don't make their own. A homemade one is better than the best store-bought one, and even more importantly, the house fills with the scent of spices and booze. This recipe has evolved over the years and produces the most moist Christmas pudding you'll ever taste.

ALE-SOAKED ENGLISH CHRISTMAS PUDDING

serves 10, with plenty left over until New Years!

7oz (200g) dried fruit (cranberries, apples, sour cherries, pears, figs)

3oz (75g) each of raisins, muscatel ideally, and currants

3½oz (100g) golden raisins

1 cup dark, fruity ale

3 tbsp rum or whiskey

juice and zest of 1 small orange and 1 small lemon

3¼oz (85g) prunes, soaked overnight in black tea

½ large banana

½ large tart dessert apple

¾ cup (1½ sticks) butter, softened

9oz (250g) dark brown sugar

1½ tbsp molasses

2 large eggs

¾ cup self-rising flour, sifted

¼ tsp ground ginger

½ tsp each of ground cinnamon and pumpkin pie spice

pinch salt

6oz (175g) white breadcrumbs

2½oz (70g) mixed candied peel

3oz (85g) nuts (Brazil nuts and toasted hazelnuts, chopped)

1 Quarter the larger pieces of dried fruit, then put them all in a bowl with the raisins, currants, and sultanas and soak overnight in the ale with the rum or whiskey and the citrus juices. The next day, drain the prunes, chop them, and add them to the mixture. Mash the banana and grate the apple, including the skin, and add to the fruit.

2 Beat the butter and sugar until light and fluffy. Add the citrus zests and molasses and beat in the eggs, one at a time. Fold in the flour, dry spices, and salt, then add the fruit with all its soaking liquor. Mix and add the breadcrumbs, mixed candied peel, and nuts.

3 Put into a greased 3-pint dessert bowl with a rim. Put together 2 large rectangles of greaseproof paper, and the same size of tin foil. Keeping them on top of each other, fold them over in the middle so that you have a pleat. Put on top of the bowl, folding it down at the sides, and tie the cover on tightly with string. Make a string handle and tie it to the sides so that you can easily lift the bowl. Trim the tin foil and greaseproof so that there are about 1½ inches (4cm) left below the level of the string—you don't want to let the covering touch the water while steaming or you'll get a soggy dessert.

4 Lower the bowl into a large pan of simmering water—to come one third of the way up the side of the dessert bowl—cover, and steam for 8 hours. Make sure that the pan does not boil dry—you'll need to top it up with boiling water from time to time.

5 Once the dessert has steamed, remove the covering and put tin foil or plastic wrap on top. Keep it somewhere cool and "feed" it every few days with good pours of whiskey or rum (or both) until Christmas Day. To serve, cover in the same way as before and steam again until warmed through (about 2 hours). Serve with cream or brandy butter.

Damsons and gin go so well together. This is a cinch to make and an exquisite color. Use plums when damsons aren't in season.

DAMSON AND GIN SORBET

serves 8

⅔ cup superfine sugar

1lb 10oz (750g) damsons (or plums)

2 tbsp gin

2 tbsp crème de cassis

1 Heat ½ cup water and the sugar gently together until the sugar has melted. Boil for 4 minutes, then leave to cool.

2 It's impossible to pit damsons so put them in a saucepan with 2 tbsp of water and cook until the fruit is completely soft. Push the fruit through a sieve to purée it and separate the pits. Mix the fruit with the sugar syrup, gin, and cassis and leave to cool completely.

3 Churn in an ice cream machine, or put in a shallow metal container in the freezer and beat the mixture 3 times during the freezing process to break up the crystals.

If Russian literature is anything to go by, the pantries in middle-class homes, pre-Revolution, must have been treasure troves. I imagine glistening jars and bottles of fruit, cordials, and homemade liqueurs, or *nastoika*, which Russians adore. Drink this straight or use it to make a Russian-style kir. My Polish friend, Kasia, swears that plum vodka in hot tea keeps colds away—any old excuse…

RUSSIAN PLUM VODKA

makes about 7 cups

2lb 4oz (1kg) red or purple plums

3½ cups granulated sugar

6½ cups vodka

1 Halve the plums but don't take the pits out. Put them into a container that will hold 7 cups (3 pints) and pour over the sugar and the vodka. Cover tightly and shake to distribute the sugar.

2 Leave to stand in a cool, dark place for about 6 weeks, turning the container occasionally to keep mixing in the sugar.

3 Strain the liquid through a piece of muslin and put into clean bottles. You can use the plums as a boozy dessert with cream or, puréed and mixed with cream, as a cake filling.

Of all the cakes I have eaten in Austria and Hungary—the full panoply of complex, layered confections such as Dobos Torte and Sacher Torte—it was the homely offerings that really stole my heart. Both yeasted and unyeasted versions of these glossy crimson squares exist, but I like these best. The recipe is based on the one they use at the glorious Café Sperl in Vienna. Eat as you would for afternoon tea—or *Jause*—in a Viennese coffee house, with cups of *mélange* (cappuccino, Viennese-style), served on a polished metal tray.

CAFÉ SPERL'S PLUM SQUARES

makes 16–20, depending on how you cut them up

2 cups all-purpose flour

½ cup (1 stick) butter

¾ cup superfine sugar

salt

1 egg yolk

1 tsp vanilla extract

1lb 8oz (675g) plums

2 tbsp granulated sugar

about 1 cup redcurrant jelly or apricot glaze

1 Preheat the oven to 350°F (180°C). Put the flour and butter into a food processor with a plastic blade attachment. Process until the mixture resembles breadcrumbs. Add the sugar and salt and mix again. Add the yolk and vanilla and keep the machine running until the mixture forms into a ball of pastry—you shouldn't need any more liquid, but you can add a drop of very cold water if the pastry isn't coming together. Wrap in plastic wrap and chill for 30 minutes.

2 Halve the plums and remove the pits. If they're small, leave them as they are, but large ones should be quartered. Press the pastry into a baking tray measuring 8 x 12 inches (20 x 30cm). Lay the plums on top in rows, pressing them lightly into the pastry. Sprinkle with the granulated sugar and bake in the preheated oven for 45 minutes.

3 Leave to cool completely, then melt the jelly or apricot glaze in a pan with a little water. Spoon the glaze on top of the plums and leave to set, then cut into squares.

"A genuine, central-European Jause consists of several large cups of coffee, topped off with whipped cream, of bread and butter, Torte or Guglhupf...It is a feminine institution; my mother didn't mind skipping lunch and dinner but she had to have her Jause. She would often complain that she gained weight 'practically from nothing,' but it couldn't be the Jause."

BLUE TROUT AND BLACK TRUFFLES JOSEPH WECHSBERG

"No fire without fir and birch, no food without horseradish and cabbage."

RUSSIAN FOLK SAYING

WINTER ON YOUR TONGUE
herbs, spices, and sour cream

It was snowing so badly on our journey from Copenhagen airport that news reports threatened road closures. Skaters were flying around the outdoor ice rink in the central square, and a little kiosk was doing a roaring trade selling glögg, the Scandinavian mulled wine rich with almonds and raisins. Given the weather and the late hour, we decided to see what room service in the hotel could rustle up. Half an hour later, they brought a tray laden with hot slices of pork belly on caraway-scented rye bread, spiced pickled prunes, cucumber, warm potatoes in sour cream and dill, and glasses of cold, golden beer: flavors of winter in a northern climate.

Many spices and herbs used in the North come from hot-weather countries. Even dill, the most prominent flavoring in Scandinavian food, is native to the Mediterranean and is used with abandon in Turkey and Iran. But warm-country flavorings have long been used in cold climates. Walking along the streets of Stockholm or Copenhagen, your nose is alert to the scent of cardamom, cinnamon, and caraway emanating from the yeasted pastries in the cafés and *Konditórei*. In Austria, aniseed and caraway speckles pork casseroles and roasted root vegetables, and in Scandinavia it flavors schnapps and rye bread. Horseradish, which we British only get out to partner roast beef, is mixed with cranberries, bread, and beets to make Russian sauces for boiled beef and roast pork. On the Swedish *smörgåsbord* table, that tongue-tingling mixture of hot and cold dishes, allspice, mustard, and horseradish are used in marinades for herrings, and all over Scandinavia you find salmon cured under a snowdrift of salt and sugar and fronds of head-clearing dill. Look at caraway seeds, ginger, and cardamom on a balmy day, and you'll be transported to India or Morocco; on days when you can see your breath in the freezing air, they take us to Scandinavia, Russia, Austria, Hungary, and even northern Italy.

Fruili-Venezia Giulia in northeast Italy is one of the most fascinating regions for seeing how warm-country flavorings have been harnessed in a cold climate. The food is unlike that from any other region of Italy. The country has been home to three great spice ports, Genoa, Venice, and Trieste. The Genoese never welcomed foreign spices into their kitchens and just a few appear in Venetian dishes, but Friuli-Venezia Giulia embraced exotic flavors, many of them coming from Trieste, a port of entry and exit for all the spices used in the Austro-Hungarian empire. It's hardly surprising a few of them were incorporated into the area's cooking.

Snowed in one Christmas in Fruili, it was hard to be sure exactly where I was, as I enjoyed goulash of beef cheeks spiced with Hungarian paprika, cabbage flavored with caraway seeds, and hams cured with juniper berries. Here, little bread dumplings are accompanied by a sauce of cucumber, sour cream, paprika, and dill, cloves flavor onions, and pasta is served with ricotta dusted with cinnamon. Horseradish is a signature flavoring of this part of northeast Italy, too. Look for a sandwich in this area, and you're more likely to find a poppy seed roll filled with ham and freshly grated horseradish than a tomato-and-mozzarella-stuffed panini.

Friuli is the only part of Italy where poppy seeds, so prevalent in the baking of eastern and central Europe, are widely used. You can enjoy them here in chocolate cakes rich with cinnamon and cloves, sprinkled over pasta and gnocchi, and used as a filling for strudel, another northern import. Central Europeans make cakes so dense with poppy seeds that they are almost black. They mix them with sour cherries, cream cheese, or apple to fill strudels, and *biegli*, little Christmas pastries stuffed with a dense honey, walnut, and poppy-seed paste, which are a speciality of Hungary. For the best flavor—a slightly musty nuttiness—pulverize poppy seeds in a coffee grinder: using them this way will bring a bit of a *mittel*-European mystery to your cooking.

Stand in the covered market in Budapest, and it's hard to believe Hungarians ever cook with anything other than their five grades of paprika. Bright strings of dried chilies fringe every stall, and the powder, the color of blood, bricks, rust, and roses, comes in scarlet tins and little red-and-green cloth sacks. It is thought paprika was brought to Hungary either by the Turks, who occupied the country in the 17th century, or by ethnic groups from the Balkans, who were fleeing north from the Turks. Enchanted by the color, Hungarian cooks started to experiment with paprika and discovered that when meat rubbed with it came into contact with heat during frying it formed a crusty brown surface that tasted like meat roasted over an open fire, which they love.

Juniper, that herby, bitter-sweet berry, makes me think of Christmas; perhaps it is the pine-tree-like bushes on which it grows. The small, purple-black berries thrive all over northern Europe as well as the Mediterranean, and from France to Finland they are used in marinades for game, in terrines and sausages, and in *après-ski* braises of beef and venison. The Finns like a strong juniper flavor—they rub chickens with pine needles and handfuls of crushed juniper berries and leave them hanging for a couple of days to mature before roasting them. Juniper is lovely cooked with cabbage, the former's ginlike herbiness lending the leaves a sophistication.

Some familiar flavorings, such as ginger, allspice, cinnamon, cardamom, and dill, can be given a new slant by looking at how they are treated in other cool climates. Dill, for example, is a comforting, nonassertive herb. Its name comes from the Norse *dilla*, meaning "to lull", and it is the main ingredient in gripe water, the old-fashioned remedy for colicky babies. This herb brings a lovely snow-fresh feel to potato and fish gratins, braised or roast chicken, buttered carrots, and dishes of onions, cabbage, and beets. Use it in big handfuls and always add it at the end of cooking time. Or try caraway seeds, once popular in Britain in breads and cakes, and now a signature flavoring in Austria, Hungary and Alsace, rubbed into roast pork or fried with potatoes.

Sour cream speaks of Scandinavia and eastern Europe more loudly than perhaps any other ingredient. It's thicker than regular cream and has a richness offset by acidity. It works in Scandinavian and eastern European cooking, either by complementing, or strongly contrasting with, other ingredients. Silky dill seems a natural partner for its tangy, clean flavor, but it's good against the richness of smoked fish, the hot sweetness of paprika and the melting powderiness of potatoes. Scandinavians like simplicity in food, and if you can make a sauce by stirring herbs or freshly grated horseradish into cream, they won't do anything more complicated. Of course, Scandinavians and eastern Europeans use sour cream just as much in the summer as in the winter, but I think of sour cream as a classic cold-weather ingredient, whispering of freshness and snow.

This dish, adapted from *The Classic Italian Cookbook* by Marcella Hazan, is fabulous. The pot-roasted lamb becomes so succulent, and the whole joint is infused with juniper berries. I was skeptical about this recipe when I first cooked it: the length of cooking time, the simplicity—would it work? But I've now been cooking this lamb for about 15 years, and everyone loves it. Don't feel daunted by the idea that you have to turn the joint every 45 minutes; just cook it on a day when you're relaxing around the house. After all, turning the meat is the only effort this dish requires.

MELTING LEG OF LAMB
with juniper berries

serves 6–8

5lb 6oz (2.4kg) leg of lamb, bone-in

1 carrot, diced

1 celery stalk, diced

½ onion, roughly chopped

2½ tsp juniper berries, crushed

3 garlic cloves, bashed with a knife

4 sprigs fresh rosemary

1½ cups white wine

salt and pepper

1 Put the lamb and all the other ingredients into a heavy-bottomed casserole dish with a lid. Set it on a low heat on the stove and cook, turning the meat every 45 minutes, for about 4 hours. By this time the lamb will have given off quite a lot of liquid.

2 Put the lid on so that it is not completely covering the meat and cook for another 1–1½ hours at a slightly higher heat, again turning the meat every 45 minutes. At the end of cooking time the meat should be completely tender and melting and brown on the outside, with some juices left in the bottom of the saucepan. If you find you have a lot of liquid, or that the meat is not brown, turn the heat up more.

3 Tilt the pan and skim off as much fat from the juices as you can. You can strain the juices to separate them from the vegetables and serve with fresh ones, or eat the juices along with the vegetables. Carve the meat and serve with the cooking juices and vegetables.

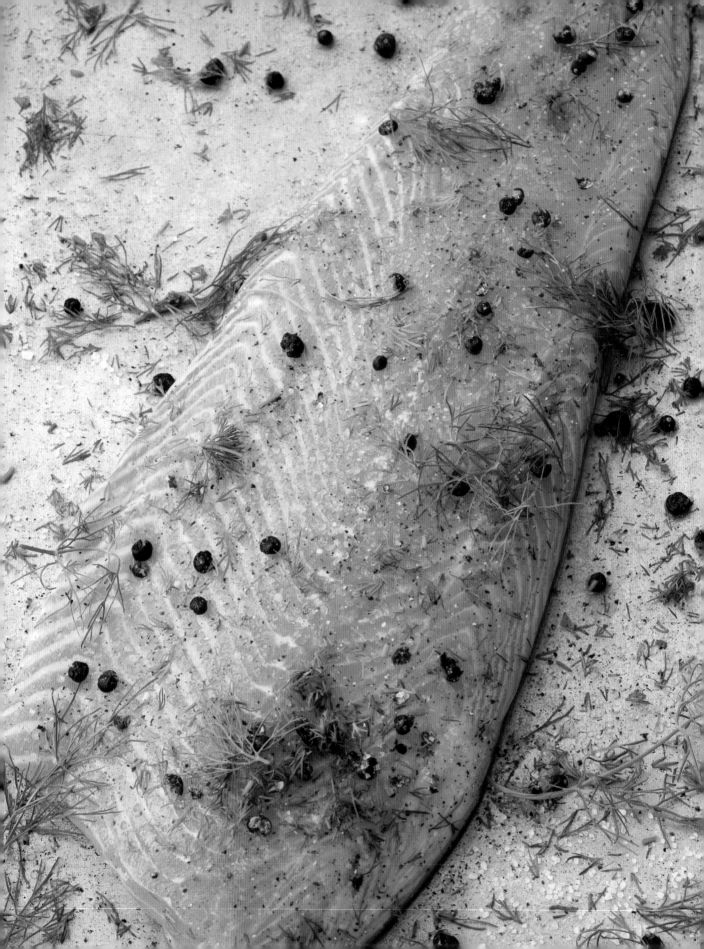

Gravlax is probably the best-known Scandinavian dish. The Swedes have a saying that gravlax should be made in silence, in coolness, and in shadow. The dish certainly seems to encapsulate the spirit of Scandinavian food—it combines the tang of the sea with greenery; the freshness of dill brings a breath of pine forests into the kitchen, and the dish smacks of the natural world and a clean, simple approach to cooking.

GIN-AND-JUNIPER-CURED SALMON
with apple and fennel cream

serves at least 10

for the cured salmon:

3lb 5oz (1.5kg) piece of salmon (preferably organic) in 2 halves, fileted but skin left on

1 tbsp chopped fennel fronds (from the heads below)

8 tbsp gin

¼ cup coarse sea salt

⅓ cup superfine sugar

2 tbsp freshly ground black pepper

1 tbsp chopped fresh dill

¾ tbsp crushed juniper berries

for the cream:
(makes enough for 10–12)

2 small heads fennel

2 small tart apples

1½ cups sour cream

2 tsp superfine sugar

5 tsp wholegrain mustard

big squeeze lemon (optional)

1 Run your hand over the salmon flesh to make sure there are no little bones in it. If there are, remove them with tweezers.

2 Spread out a piece of tin foil big enough to wrap around the salmon. Rub gin all over the 2 pieces of salmon and set 1 piece of it on the tin foil skin-side-down. Pour a little more gin over the fleshy side of the salmon, then mix the salt, sugar, pepper, fennel, dill, and juniper berries and press this on top of the salmon. Sprinkle with a little gin. Put the other piece of salmon on top, skin-side-up. Sprinkle a little more gin on top.

3 Fold the tin foil around the salmon to make a package. Set it on a wire rack and put this on a platter or a roasting tray that can catch the liquid as it leaches out of the salmon. Place a weight such as a cutting board on top and put in the fridge. Turn the salmon package from time to time while it is curing. You can leave it for anything from 1–6 days.

4 To make the cream, remove any tough outer leaves from the fennel and trim the ends. Cut the bulb into quarters lengthways and carefully slice the central core out of each piece. Cut the fennel into fine strips, about the length of your index finger. Halve and core the apple (you can peel it, too, if you like) and cut it into strips. Mix the fennel and apple with the sour cream, sugar, and mustard, taste, and add a squeeze of lemon if you wish. Cover and keep in the fridge.

5 Unwrap the package and scrape the salt and sugar off the salmon. Using a very sharp knife, cut the salmon flesh horizontally into thin slices, leaving the skin behind. Serve with the apple and fennel cream and thin slices of buttered rye or pumpernickel bread.

ZAKUSKI

Zakuski is a spread of Russian appetizers, little dishes that, rather like Mediterranean *mezze*, can either start a meal or constitute the entire thing. I suppose they're a kind of Russian *smörgåsbord*. The flavors used are indeed very Scandinavian, and Georgian dishes and ingredients, which Russians love, are prominent as well.

You don't need many *zakuski* to make a meal, especially as the idea is to supplement them with foods you can buy. Bread is obligatory. Middle Eastern flatbread is good with Georgian flavors; rye is better with more Russian ones, so have a little of both. Radishes—especially the long, white-tipped French breakfast variety, if you're able to find them—make perfect, slightly peppery little dippers, and fingers of cucumber are good, too. Cured herring and good smoked fish are an easy way to extend the range, and Georgian cheese pies—you'll find a recipe on page 15—are always served with the *zakuski* spread in Georgian restaurants in Russia. Spicy sausage and cured ham give you your protein fix, and olives and pickled chilies (available in Middle Eastern shops or grocery store speciality sections) are a must. For extra glamour, add hard-boiled eggs—either quails' or hens'—warm waxy potatoes, little bowls of sour cream, and salmon caviar. Provide bottles of viscous ice-cold vodka and get ready to dispense a bit of Russian hospitality. *"Prosim k stolu!"* as they say there, or "Please, to the table".

the recipes as a group serve 8 as a *zakuski* spread, but could stretch to 10–12 with the addition of some simple store-bought ingredients

2 tbsp butter

1lb (450g) mushrooms, cleaned and finely chopped

¾ tsp cayenne pepper

4 scallions, chopped

salt and pepper

good squeeze lemon

¾ cup sour cream

chopped fresh dill

mushroom caviar

1 Heat the butter in a frying pan and, once it's foaming, add the mushrooms. Sauté briskly so that the mushrooms get some color, then add the cayenne and scallions and seasoning of salt and pepper, and cook until the mushrooms have exuded their liquid and this has evaporated. Add a good squeeze of lemon and the sour cream. Turn the heat down and let the sour cream combine with the mushroom flavors, but don't let the mixture boil.

2 Take the pan off the heat, add the dill, and check the seasoning. You can serve this lukewarm or at room temperature. The dish doesn't taste so good if it's been in the fridge, so cook it near to the time you want it serve it.

7oz (200g) smoked fish (see introduction for types)

¼ cup (½ stick) unsalted butter, softened

yolks of 2 hard-boiled eggs

good squeeze of lemon

pepper

½ tsp creamed horseradish, or to taste

smoked fish and horseradish butter

You can use mackerel, smoked herring, or smoked salmon trimmings for this butter.

1 If you are using fish that has skin, remove it. Either mash the fish with the butter and egg using a fork or roughly purée it in a food processor using the pulse button. The texture depends on how coarse or smooth you like it, but you don't want baby food. Add lemon, pepper, and creamed horseradish to taste.

7oz (200g) feta cheese

⅔ cup sour cream

1 small garlic clove, crushed

¼ tsp cayenne pepper

½ tbsp chopped fresh dill or a mixture fresh dill and tarragon

handful black olives in olive oil, to serve

pot cheese

Use Greek yogurt instead of sour cream if you prefer.

1 Simply mash together all the ingredients (except the olives). Put some olives, drained of their oil, on top before serving.

9oz (250g) cooked kidney beans (drained weight)

1 tbsp olive oil

salt and pepper

good squeeze of lemon

for the plum sauce:

5½oz (150g) plums

2oz (50g) pitted prunes

2 tbsp dark brown sugar

¼ cup red wine vinegar

¼ tsp cayenne pepper (or more to taste)

1 garlic clove, crushed

2 tbsp mixture fresh cilantro and mint, roughly chopped

Georgian beans in plum sauce

This dish, *lobio tkemali*, combines two great Georgian loves, beans and plum sauce. The recipe makes rather more plum sauce than you need, but it's hard to deal with smaller quantities and it's also great with fried chicken or lamb kebobs.

1 For the plum sauce, halve the plums and remove the pits. Put all the ingredients for the plum sauce, except the herbs, with ¼ cup water into a saucepan and bring to the boil. Immediately turn down to a simmer and cook for about 20 minutes. Purée the mixture and add the chopped herbs, keeping some back for scattering on top of the dish.

2 Mix the cooked beans with the olive oil, season, add the lemon juice, and slightly mash the mixture so that some beans are broken up and others remain whole. Mix with 4 tbsp of the plum sauce. Check the seasoning, put into a bowl, and scatter with herbs.

12oz (350g) beets, either cooked or raw (but not pickled)

3oz (75g) walnut pieces

½ tsp sea salt

3 garlic cloves, crushed

2½ tbsp chopped fresh cilantro

2½ tbsp chopped fresh parsley

¼ tsp ground coriander seeds

2 tsp red wine vinegar

½ tbsp olive oil

pepper

seeds from ½ pomegranate (optional), to serve

beet, walnut, and cilantro purée

This dish, *charkhlis pkhali*, is another popular Georgian *zakuski*.

1 Preheat the oven to 375°F (190°C). If you're going to cook raw beets, don't do anything except wash them and cut off any leaves about 1½ inches (4cm) from their base. Cutting the beets will make the crimson juices run out while cooking. Wrap the beets in tin foil, place in a small roasting tray and bake for 1½ hours, or until tender, in the oven.

2 Meanwhile, grind together the walnuts, salt, and garlic, either in a mortar and pestle or in a food processor using the pulse button. Add the fresh herbs and continue grinding until you have a paste.

3 When the beets are cool enough to handle, peel them, grate the flesh into a bowl, and mix in the walnut paste and the remaining ingredients (except the pomegranate seeds). Keep the mixture in the fridge but bring to room temperature before serving. Pomegranate seeds look beautiful scattered over the top.

Tafelspitz is much more than boiled beef. Made well and served with the classic accompaniments, apple and horseradish sauce or chive sauce, it is one of the glories of Viennese cookery. The restaurant Meissl & Schaden, once a Viennese institution, used to list 24 different boiled beef specialties on its menu and kept its own herds of cattle just outside Vienna, feeding them on molasses and mashed sugar beet. Boiled beef is no longer, as the epicure Joseph Wechsburg has written, "a way of life", not just a dish, but it is still hugely popular. If you baulk at the idea of eating *apfelkren*, or apple sauce, with beef, then serve creamed horseradish instead, just as you would with roast beef, but the apple and horseradish sauce is a revelation. *Tafelspitz* itself is actually a particular cut, taken from the rump, but it's difficult to get hold of and even Viennese restaurants now use other cuts.

AUSTRIAN TAFELSPITZ
with apple sauce

3 beef bones

4lb 8oz (2kg) beef in one piece, such as silverside or brisket

2 large carrots, quartered

2 leeks, cleaned and quartered

½ small celeriac, peeled

2 medium onions, stuck with 2 cloves

parsley and bay leaf, tied to ½ celery stalk

¼oz (10g) dried wild mushrooms

1 tsp black peppercorns

a few chives

for the apple sauce (*apfelkren*):

1lb (450g) cooking apples

2 tbsp granulated sugar

3 tbsp freshly grated horseradish

1½ tbsp white wine vinegar

salt and pepper

1 Scald the beef bones with boiling water, then rinse in cold water. Put the bones into a heavy casserole dishn that will accommodate everything, cover with water, bring to the boil and simmer for half an hour. Add the beef and, when the water returns to simmering, skim the surface. Put in the rest of the ingredients and add more water to cover if you need to. Simmer, with the water only just trembling, for 2½ hours (or until cooked), skimming every so often.

2 Make the sauce while the beef is cooking. Peel, core, and chop the apples and cook them in a saucepan with the sugar and a splash of water. Mash them into a lumpy purée. Leave them to cool, then add the horseradish and vinegar. Taste and season.

3 Lift the beef carefully out of its broth—it will be very tender— and cut it into thick slices across the grain. Put onto a heated platter, moisten with some of the cooking broth, and scatter with chives. Serve with the sauce on the side. Creamed spinach and a few root vegetables are the ideal accompaniments.

Salted herring, marinated in vinegar, sugar, spices, sour cream, onions, mustard, and dill, are the stars of the *smörgåsbord* table. You can get salted herring from a good fish counter, or substitute *matjes* herring, available in jars and tins. To prepare your own, make a brine, dissolving ¼ cup salt per 1 pint (2½ cups) water, and immerse fresh herring filets in this for 3 hours—you do not need to soak these before use.

SCANDINAVIAN CURED HERRING

serves 6–8

1½lb (675g) salted herring filets

milk and water to cover fish

¾ cup white wine vinegar

¼ cup superfine sugar

2 tsp each whole allspice and yellow mustard seeds

3 bay leaves

1 medium carrot

¼ inch (5mm) square piece ginger

1¾-inch (4-cm) long piece horseradish root

2 small red onions

glassblower's herring

1 Soak the salted herring in a mixture of milk and water (half and half) for 2 hours, then wash them under cold running water.

2 Put the vinegar, ½ cup water, the sugar, allspice, mustard, and bay leaves in a saucepan and bring slowly to the boil, stirring to help the sugar dissolve. Remove from the heat and leave to cool completely.

3 Peel and julienne the carrot, ginger, and horseradish, doing the latter two finely. Finely slice the onions. Cut the herring into 2-inch (5-cm) long pieces and layer them up in a glass preserving jar with the carrots, onions, ginger and horseradish, pouring on the spiced vinegar as you go. The liquid should just cover the fish. Put the lid on, refrigerate, and eat after 2–3 days, with warm potatoes or rye bread.

1lb (450g) salted herring filets

milk and water to cover fish

½ small onion

3 tbsp chopped scallions

1 cup sour cream

1 tsp each Dijon mustard and cayenne pepper

1 tbsp superfine sugar

3 tbsp chopped fresh dill

herring with sour cream

1 Soak and cut the herring filets as in point 1 above.

2 Finely slice the onion. Mix it with all the other ingredients and combine with the fish. Cover loosely, put in the fridge, and leave to chill overnight. Serve as you would glassblower's herring.

Budapest is wild. I went there for the pastries and ended up loving it for Hungary's savory food—the big, unarguable-with flavors of pork, peppers, and paprika—and the riotous behavior of the natives when they've knocked back a bit too much plum brandy. The night we arrived we went straight to a little restaurant someone had recommended. The taxi dropped us off in what appeared to be a concrete wasteland, but once inside Kehil we were seduced by the gypsy music, the clapping and dancing (done not by performers but by the customers), the impromptu and tearful rendition of Hungarian ballads, and the constant flow of alcohol. There wasn't a tourist in sight; Kehil is a real neighborhood restaurant. It doesn't make many concessions to tourist palates, either; the menu was full of classic Hungarian dishes, with paprika used in all its variations, sauerkraut, dumplings, and even some rather frightening-sounding dishes such as Transylvanian stew (the mind boggles) and bear's paw (actually a huge breaded pork chop that had been heavily marinated in garlic). This is where I also became acquainted with *lecsó*, the Hungarian ratatouille that is served hot or at room temperature, on its own or with sausages or other pork dishes (it's great with pork chops). I'm not a big lover of green peppers, but I was knocked out by this fantastic dinner dish.

HUNGARIAN LECSÓ

serves 4

1 tbsp sunflower or peanut oil

1 large onion, sliced

1lb 2oz (500g) mixed red and green peppers, finely sliced

1lb 2oz (500g) tomatoes, chopped

½ tbsp sweet paprika

½–1 tsp hot paprika, or to taste

½ tbsp granulated sugar

salt and pepper

sour cream, to serve

1 Heat the oil in a frying pan and cook the onion over a low heat for 5 minutes until softening, then add the peppers. Cook for 10–15 minutes, stirring frequently, until the peppers have really softened and then tip in the tomatoes, both kinds of paprika, sugar, and seasoning of salt and pepper. Mix everything together and cook over a medium heat for about 25 minutes, stirring often. The mixture should be completely soft and sloppy and neither too dry nor too wet (something akin to ratatouille).

2 Check the seasoning. Serve the *lecsó* on its own, topped with sour cream, or with broad egg noodles, such as pappardelle, or rice.

"Gilded apples and walnuts hung in clusters as if they grew there, and a hundred little white, blue, and even red, candles were fastened to its twigs... And up at its very top was set a large gold tinsel star. It was splendid, I tell you, splendid beyond all words!"

THE FIR TREE HANS CHRISTIAN ANDERSEN

All cold-weather countries revel in the baking that goes with Christmas and New Year festivities. I have Swedish friends who start preparing for Christmas right at the beginning of December; I suppose it is a way of getting through the darkness. Here are three sweet treats from the plethora cooked every year.

SNOW COOKIES

makes 24

½ cup (1 stick) butter

½ cup confectioners sugar

¼ tsp salt

1 small egg yolk

1½ cups all-purpose flour

to finish:

1 cup confectioners sugar, sifted

vodka or water

lemon juice

edible gold powder (available from specialist cake-decorating shops or online)

Danish gilded stars

1 Beat the butter, sugar, and salt together until combined. Mix in the egg yolk. Mix the flour in by hand and bring the dough together in a ball, kneading lightly. Wrap in plastic wrap and refrigerate overnight.

2 Preheat the oven to 350°F (180°C). Roll the dough out to ⅛ inch (3mm) thick. Stamp out cookies with a star-shaped cookie cutter and put them on to a baking tray. Bake for 8 minutes. Leave to cool on a wire cooling rack.

3 Put the confectioners sugar into a bowl and add enough vodka (or water) and lemon juice to make a frosting that you can drizzle: scoop up some frosting on the tines of a fork and if it drops in a slow but steady stream, it is the right consistency. Drizzle onto the cookies. When the frosting is nearly set, carefully sprinkle the cookies with edible gold powder.

Scandinavian *pepparkakor*

makes about 24

¼ cup (½ stick) butter

⅓ cup light brown sugar

2 tbsp milk

1 tbsp molasses

2 cups all-purpose flour

¼ tbsp ground cinnamon

1 tsp ground ginger

½ tsp ground cardamom

1 tsp finely grated orange zest

½ tsp bicarbonate of soda

to decorate (optional):

1 egg white, confectioners sugar, and squeeze of lemon

This is *the* Christmas cookie throughout Scandinavia. You can finish them simply by drizzling frosting over them or, if you want to be more ambitious, make a firm royal frosting (you just have to add more sifted confectioners sugar) and get your piping bag and nozzle out. You can put people's names on them as they do in Finland, or just leave them completely unfrosted as they often do in Sweden.

1 Cream the butter and sugar in a mixer. Add the milk and molasses and blend until smooth. Stir in all the other ingredients and bring together in a ball. Continue as in the recipe for Danish gilded stars (see page 160), cutting the cookies into festive shapes, such as hearts, stars, moons, and candy canes, and baking for about 8 minutes.

2 To decorate the cookies, mix the egg white with enough sifted confectioners sugar to make a firm paste. Either decorate simply by drizzling lines of this across the cookies using the tines of a fork, or use a piping set and frost them more fancily.

Russian snow twigs

makes 24

2 large eggs and 1 egg yolk

1 tbsp heavy cream

4 tbsp superfine sugar

¼ tsp salt

2 tbsp vodka or brandy

3 cups all-purpose flour, sifted

½ tsp baking powder

sunflower or vegetable oil for deep-frying

confectioners sugar

These are lovely at a Christmas party, bringing a real festive air to the proceedings. You do need a couple of friends to help with the last-minute frying, though, or you'll be standing at the stove all night: the demand for them never seems to abate.

1 Beat together the whole eggs, egg yolk, cream, and sugar and add the salt and vodka or brandy.

2 Gradually sprinkle on the flour and baking powder. Mix to a dough and knead lightly. Roll out into a rectangle about ⅛ inch (3mm) thick. Cut into strips about the width of 1½ fingers and 3 inches (8cm) long.

3 Heat the oil in a deep pan until a piece of bread dropped into it sizzles and turns golden in about a minute. Deep-fry the twigs, being careful not to overcrowd the pan, until they are light golden. Drain on paper towel, dust generously with confectioners sugar, and serve immediately.

I drank so much mulled wine while researching this book—in town squares, cafés, homes, and ski slopes in Austria, northern Italy, Hungary, France, Denmark, and Sweden. I was interested to see how subtly different the various offerings were and why we make often turns out stuff that tastes like something you'd buy from the drugstore. My conclusion? The spicing has to be carefully handled (easy on the cloves), the wine has to be drinkable, and you need a good bit of help from spirits. *Glögg* is mulled wine, Scandinavian-style, and this is the best version I know.

GLÖGG
mulled wine

serves 8

2 bottles fruity red wine

1 cup superfine sugar

8 cloves

8 cardamom pods, lightly crushed

1 stick cinnamon

peel of 1 orange (cut away the white pith)

1 cup aquavit liquor

3oz (75g) raisins

1½ tbsp slivered almonds

1 tbsp Angostura bitters

1 cup Madeira or Marsala

really generous pour Cointreau or other orange liqueur

1 Put the wine into a large saucepan with the sugar. Gently heat, stirring to help the sugar dissolve.

2 Put the spices and the orange peel in a little muslin bag and add this to the wine. Add all the other ingredients and simmer on a low heat for 15 minutes or so, but don't let the mixture boil.

3 Serve in glasses with small spoons so that people can scoop out and eat the almonds and the boozy raisins.

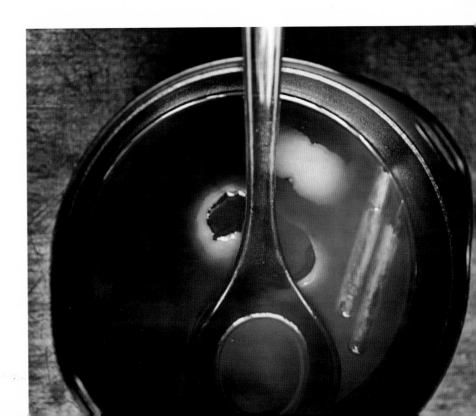

Bugnes, little deep-fried pastry bows, are from Lyons, but they appear in Annecy in the Savoie every year once the weather gets cold. There they add Chartreuse to the hot chocolate, but I prefer brandy and I like it added to the cream, not the hot chocolate. Good-quality creamy milk really makes a difference to this drink, as does top-quality chocolate powder or flakes.

SKIER'S CHOCOLATE
with *bugnes*

serves 6–8

1 cup heavy cream

2 tbsp confectioners sugar

4 tbsp brandy

3½oz (100g) cocoa

4¾ cups whole milk

for the *bugnes*:

3 cups all-purpose flour

1½ tsp baking powder

¼ cup superfine sugar

½ tsp salt

¼ cup (½ stick) butter, melted and cooled

3 medium eggs, lightly beaten

1 tbsp brandy or rum

grated rind of 1 lemon

sunflower or vegetable oil for deep-frying

confectioners sugar for dusting

1 tsp cinnamon for dusting

1 You can make the *bugnes* mixture up to 24 hours in advance and deep-fry them at the last minute. Sift three quarters of the flour into a bowl with the baking powder, sugar, and salt. Mix the butter, eggs, brandy or rum, and lemon rind in a bowl. Make a well in the center of the flour and add the liquid gradually, mixing as you do so. Bring together the dough—it will be very sticky—and knead it, working in the remaining flour. Turn out onto a floured surface and knead for 3 minutes, until it is very smooth. Cover and leave for half an hour.

2 Roll the dough out to ⅛ inch (2mm) thick and cut it into rectangles 6 x 2½ inches (15 x 6.5cm). Cut a slit, lengthways, in the middle of each rectangle so you have ¾ inch (2cm) of dough on either side at the top and bottom. Put one end of the pastry strip through the slit so you are left with slightly twisted edges. This will make them look like little bows when fried. Set on a floured tray, cover, and chill for an hour.

3 Whip the cream, adding the sugar and gradually the brandy or rum. Be careful not to overbeat; you want luxurious folds. Put the drinking chocolate in a pan and add enough boiling water just to cover it. Put on a low heat and melt the chocolate, stirring. Add the milk and bring to the boil. You can quickly reheat this once the pastries are ready.

4 To cook the *bugnes*, heat the oil to 375°F (190°C) and deep-fry 3–4 at a time, turning them over when they are brown on one side. They cook quickly, so don't take your eyes off them. Lift them out with a slotted spoon onto paper towels. Sift with confectioners sugar and cinnamon and serve with the hot chocolate topped with the brandy (or rum) cream.

All Scandinavian countries have special Christmas breads; they are as important as Christmas cake or gingerbread houses. My only problem was which one to select. The Danes are widely regarded as the best bakers in Scandinavia, so here is their Christmas offering. The flavor of cardamom, as with a lot of Danish baking, is pretty dominant. Have your kringle with mulled wine or strong coffee and don't forget to light a few candles while you're eating. That's what the Danes would do, to enjoy a bit of *hygge*, their great concept of cosiness and well-being.

DANISH CHRISTMAS KRINGLE
with cardamom

makes 1 loaf to feed about 8 greedy people

2 tsp dried yeast

2 tbsp superfine sugar

⅓ cup warm milk

2½ cups bread flour

pinch salt

seeds from 20 cardamom pods, crushed

½ cup (1 stick) butter, melted

1 medium egg, beaten

for the filling:

½ cup butter (1 stick), softened

4 tbsp light brown sugar

1oz (30g) sliced almonds

1oz (30g) dried cranberries

1½oz (40g) fresh cranberries

to finish:

1 egg, beaten

½oz (15g) slivered almonds

5 sugar cubes, roughly crushed

½ cup confectioners sugar

lemon juice and water

1 Mix the yeast with 1 tsp sugar and cover with some of the warm milk. Leave in a warm place for about 15 minutes, until it is frothing.

2 Put the flour, salt, cardamom, and the rest of the sugar in a bowl. Make a well in the middle and pour in the yeast mixture, the melted butter, and the beaten egg. Gradually bring all the flour into the well of wet ingredients and add the remaining milk a little at a time—you might not need all of it. You want a dough that is soft but not too sticky. Knead well, lightly oil a bowl, and put the dough into it. Cover loosely and leave somewhere warm to double in size. Mix all the ingredients for the filling together and set aside.

3 Preheat the oven to 400°F (200°C). When the dough has risen, knock it back and roll out on a lightly floured surface into a strip measuring about 34 x 4 inches (85 x 10cm). Spread the filling down the center of this, then fold in the 2 ends of the long sides on top of one another so that you are left with a parcel.

4 Lightly butter a baking tray and put the dough on it. Shape the two ends around to form a giant pretzel shape. Cover lightly again with plastic wrap and leave in a warm place to proof for 30 minutes.

5 Brush the top with the beaten egg and sprinkle with the almonds and the crushed sugar cubes. Bake in the preheated oven for 20–25 minutes, or until golden-brown. Leave to cool. Sift the confectioners sugar into a small bowl, then add just enough lemon juice and water to make a thin frosting. Drizzle the frosting over the top of the kringle.

"I enjoyed this cranberrying very much, notwithstanding the wet and cold,
and the swamp seemed to be yielding its crop to me alone...
*I would gladly share my gains, take one or twenty into partnership
and get this swamp with them, but I do not know an individual
whom this berry cheers and nourishes as it does me."*

WILD FRUITS HENRY DAVID THOREAU

FROM BUSH AND BOG
cranberries, blackberries, sloes, and rose hips

It is a freezing October in Massachusetts, and everywhere I look there are scarlet lakes surrounded by trees glowing with autumnal foliage. The beauty of cranberries, Christmas-red and smooth as beads, ebbing and flowing in blue, flooded bogs, is mesmerising. My eyes can barely cope with the color. "I love cranberry bogs when they're filled with water," says Irene Sorenson, who takes care of many of the cranberry farmers in this state, one of the biggest growing areas. "They are so romantic: irregularly shaped, curvaceous, organic." Cranberry growers, and there are only about a thousand of them worldwide, talk about their crop with love. Most of them are fifth- or sixth-generation and have berries in their blood. At this time of year, when the harvest is in full swing, they work around the clock. Some rest only by grabbing a bit of shut eye under a tree in the woods near the bogs, but they will not leave their precious fruit. In fact, most growers are so fond of cranberries that, despite their unalloyed tartness, you will see them throwing raw cranberries into the air and letting them fall into their mouths.

The cranberry is an ancient berry, indigenous to North America and, since it formed part of the first Thanksgiving meal, is a potent symbol of American beginnings and survival. It's certainly a plucky little berry. The naturally waxy coating will keep it fresh for a good three months in the bottom of the fridge, and it's also cute and endlessly cheering. The Native Americans ate cranberries fresh and used them in *pemmican*, a kind of energy bar made of preserved venison and fat. They also used the juice to dye blankets and feathers and made poultices from them, and a basket of cranberries often sat in the middle of meetings with different tribes as a sign of friendship and goodwill.

When you look at the stacks of cranberries that arrive in our shops every Christmas, it's hard to believe they haven't always been this abundant, but at one time they only grew wild. People picked them from patches near their homes, just for themselves. Commercial cultivation of cranberries only started two centuries ago, and the berries were harvested "dry", picked with long wooden combs. It was a slow and backbreaking process. Nowadays most berries are harvested "wet". The bogs where they grow are flooded and large machines with big whirling beaters, referred to as "egg beaters", are driven through the bogs and gently dislodge the berries from the vines. Because cranberries contain little air pockets, they immediately float to the surface of the water. They are then herded towards a pipe, in pools marbled in shades of crimson and salmon-pink. As most berries are destined for juice or sauce, it doesn't matter that they get so wet, but fruit to be sold fresh is still dry-harvested, collected by machines that look like large lawn mowers.

Sadly, cranberries suffer from being part of our Christmas celebrations. Once the decorations are down, we don't think about them until the following December. It's a crying shame, especially when our range of winter fruits is so limited. We could do with the cranberry's tartness and piercing color right into the spring, and they'll certainly keep that long, providing stunning sorbets and bringing bursts of flavor and brightness to crumbles, cobblers, tarts, cakes, and compotes (they are spectacular gently poached in a sugar syrup and mixed with slices of blood orange), right until the end of March.

I don't just use these berries for desserts. Cranberry sauce is great with pork. Many of the cranberry pickers in Massachusetts are of Cape Verdean origin and celebrate the end of the harvest with a hog roast accompanied by cranberry sauce. Cranberry sauce is also a fine substitute for the lingonberry sauce that is eaten with Scandinavian meat dishes and easier to make since lingonberries are almost impossible to get hold of. Cranberries are a must for Russian cooking, too. There they are made into *kissel* (a fruit compote thickened with arrowroot), find their way into tarts, are steeped in vodka to make cranberry liqueur, and are mixed with horseradish to make a relish for beef. And the Finns love them. You can see them in the market in Helsinki, bobbing in barrels of water alongside the smaller lingonberries. Dried cranberries, always slightly sweetened, are available all year round and they're perfect for bringing little nuggets of sweet-sour flavor to wild rice salads. So, the cranberry isn't just for Christmas. Buy them, freeze them, or stash them somewhere cool and enjoy their tart fruitiness right into the spring.

In England, blackberries are regarded as a fruit of the late summer and early fall. But growing up in Northern Ireland, I thought of blackberry picking as an activity for October, and a definite sign that fall was in full swing. There were still plenty of blackberries in the bushes, even after the clocks had changed. I remember coming home in the near-dark, as layers of mist settled over the fields, bearing saucepans and milk cans full of them. With hands scratched and stained, we cooked the fruit immediately. Looking at their glossy black bodies, it was hard to believe they wouldn't remain intact and beautiful, but as the poet Seamus Heaney reminds us, they don't keep. A fur starts to creep over them, he writes: "a rat-gray fungus, glutting our cache". Any hope that they would survive would be bludgeoned the next day, and you were left with a gnawing guilt that you had taken more fruit than you needed.

If you want to enjoy blackberries, you still need to pick them yourself. Those that find their way into the shops are prohibitively expensive, and anyway, blackberries are best appreciated when you have so many that you don't know what to do with them—all sweet and black and free. It is the way this abundance makes the cook's head spin that is their greatest joy.

But North American's are lucky: blackberries are widely cultivated in the United States, where the berries growing on erect, woody plants rather than sprawling bushes. Americans make so many of their great desserts with them—cobblers and buckles and slumps *et al*—that this abundance is a necessity. A "black-and-blue" cobbler, made with blackberries and blueberries, covered with a cookielike buttermilk dough, may sound boring but, with its network of crimson juices bursting through pastry, is wickedly alive.

Blackberries are popular in eastern Europe as well, though more as an accompaniment to meat than as a dessert. Georgians use them for their famous tart sauces, pushing the puréed fruit through a sieve before mixing it with garlic and chili, dill and cilantro, a great accompaniment to lamb kebobs or roast chicken, though I prefer to add a dash of sugar, too.

A simple treatment is best for blackberries. Eat them in apple and blackberry tarts, crumbles made with brown sugar and chunks of hazelnuts and walnuts, or just on their own with some heavy whipping cream and a sprinkling of sugar. Dorothy Hartley suggests a blackberry salad made by leaving the berries somewhere warm and then adding sugar and red wine just before serving, and they make a lovely simple fruit salad with chunks of ripe melon, too.

I think of rose hips as the strawberries of fall. Not that you can scoff them in the same carefree way—the seeds of the hip are covered with tiny hairs—it's just that they carry the taste of strawberries and roses. I started looking for good places to pick rose hips because I yearned to recapture the flavor of the rose hip syrup my granny kept. It wasn't such an unusual foodstuff to have around in her day. Rose hips are so full of vitamin C—they are said to contain four times as much as blackcurrants and 20 times as much as oranges—that during the Second World War children were sent to gather them to make syrup. This syrup was given as a vitamin supplement to children, and you can still buy it in health food stores.

When I first visited Scandinavia, I was amazed to see how mainstream rose hips were there. In Sweden, rose hip juice is as prominent on the drinks' shelves as orange juice. In the winter this is heated to make a warm, sweet soup, and whole berries are added to pear and apple tarts. The Russians and Poles love these little berries, too, principally as a jelly to eat with game. I like them with venison, as a topping for warm scones and to melt into warm rice pudding, and in a salad of speck and prosciutto with wild arugula. It was a dollop of rose hip jelly I had in northern Italy that made me realize how good it was with *charcuterie*.

Gather rose hips after they've been softened by the first frosts, usually around the end of October, and use them soon after picking. To make rose hip jelly, just cook washed ripe rose hips with twice their weight in cooking apples in enough water to cover. When the fruit is soft and pulpy—it will take about 45 minutes —strain it through a jelly bag overnight. Put the extracted juice in a large saucepan and add 1lb (450g) sugar for every 1 pint (2½ cups) of juice. Heat gently until the sugar has dissolved, then boil rapidly for 15 minutes, or until the setting point is reached—put a teaspoon of the hot liquid on a cold saucer and see whether it wrinkles when you push it with your finger—and store in sterilized jars. Rose hips really do carry the quintessential flavor of fall in the country for me.

Sloes, grown mainly in Great Britain, are perhaps the hardest of these autumnal berries to like. Mouth-puckeringly astringent, they are not for straightforward eating, but for dousing in gin or vodka and sugar. My uncle used to turn up with a bottle of his sloe gin every year just before Christmas, and we hoarded it as though it was vintage champagne. Tasting of blackcurrant and clove candy, it was the first alcohol I ever liked. Don't just keep it for Christmas. Added to champagne, it makes a wonderful British-style kir, and the boozy little bodies left behind after you've strained off the gin can be incorporated into a chocolate truffle mix for a sublime after-dinner treat.

My first trip to America—on my honeymoon—was arranged entirely around restaurants I wanted to eat in. In my notebook of the ingredients and dishes on offer, warm salads based on wild rice and dried cranberries turn up again and again—they seem to be a classic of modern American cooking. You can use smoked chicken or duck instead of fresh duck for this, too.

WARM DUCK AND WILD RICE SALAD
with dried cranberries and maple-cider vinaigrette

serves 6 as a starter

2oz (50g) dried cranberries

1oz (25g) pecan halves

2oz (50g) wild rice

3½oz (100g) organic brown rice

1 cup chicken stock

salt and pepper

3 duck breasts, skin on

4½oz (125g) green beans, topped and cut in half

2 tbsp roughly chopped fresh flat-leaf parsley

for the dressing:

½ tbsp cider vinegar

¼ tsp Dijon mustard

½ tbsp maple syrup

salt and pepper

2 tbsp peanut oil

2 tbsp olive oil

I Cover the cranberries with just-boiled water and leave to plump for 20 minutes. Drain. Meanwhile, make the rest of the dish.

2 Preheat the oven to 400°F (200°C). Put the pecans in a dry frying pan over a medium heat and toast them, turning them over so that they get cooked on both sides. Watch them like a hawk, though—nuts burn really quickly. Let them cool and then chop them very roughly—you want to be left with big pieces of nut.

3 Put the wild and brown rice in separate saucepans. Cover the wild rice with plenty of water and add the chicken stock to the brown rice. Simmer both until cooked. Wild rice never really softens but stays firm and nutty; it should be ready in 30 minutes. The brown rice will take 35–40 minutes; it stays nutty as well, but less so than the wild rice. The brown rice should absorb all the stock as it cooks, but make sure it doesn't go dry. Add a little water when it is needed.

4 Meanwhile, make the dressing by whisking together all the ingredients. Season the duck breasts well, then brown them in their own fat on each side, skin-side-down first. Once the breasts are browned, put them in an ovenproof dish and roast in the preheated oven for 5–7 minutes. Remove, cover, and allow to rest for 4 minutes. Cook the beans in boiling, salted water until al dente, then drain.

5 Drain the wild rice. Mix it with the brown rice, which should be quite dry, having absorbed all the stock, the beans, cranberries, pecans, and parsley. Toss everything together with the dressing and season.

6 Cut the duck breasts into slices and serve half a breast per person, laid on a mound of the dressed rice mixture.

Meatballs. The idea somehow never seems to inspire people, but I adore this recipe, a classic of Swedish home cooking. Use ground venison instead of beef if you want something with a little more punch. You can serve the meatballs with lingonberry sauce, as they do in Sweden—they stock jars of it in IKEA—but fresh lingonberries are virtually impossible to get, and cranberries are a fine substitute.

SWEDISH MEATBALLS
with cranberry sauce

serves 6

¼ cup (½ stick) butter

1 small onion, very finely chopped

2 tsp ground allspice

3½oz (100g) breadcrumbs

⅔ cup milk

2lb 4oz (1kg) ground pork and beef

1 large egg, beaten

salt and pepper

2 tbsp sunflower or peanut oil

1 tbsp all-purpose flour

1¾ cups chicken or beef stock

1 cup sour cream

3 tbsp roughly chopped fresh dill

for the cranberry sauce:

1lb 2oz (500g) cranberries

finely grated zest and juice of 1 lemon

⅔ cup superfine sugar

1 To make the cranberry sauce, simply put the cranberries in a small, heavy-bottomed saucepan with ½ cup water and the lemon juice and zest. Bring up to the boil, then turn the heat down low and cook for about 15 minutes. When the berries have started to pop, add the sugar and continue to cook until the sugar has melted. Take off the heat, taste to see if the sauce is as sweet as you want it, and leave to cool.

2 Melt 1 tbsp of the butter and in it sauté the onion until soft but not colored. Add the allspice and cook for a further minute.

3 Soak the breadcrumbs in the milk until all the milk has been absorbed—about 30 minutes. Mix the onion and the soaked breadcrumbs with the meat and egg and season really well. With wet hands, form the mixture into balls a little larger than walnuts.

4 Heat half of the remaining butter with half the oil and fry the meatballs in batches, making sure that they get a good color on the outside. Try not to burn the fat, but if you do, discard it before you fry the next set of meatballs. Put the cooked meatballs aside.

5 Heat the remaining butter and oil in the pan. Add the flour and cook over a low heat, stirring, until the flour is golden. Take the pan off the heat and gradually add the stock, stirring well after each addition. Put the pan back on the heat and, stirring constantly, bring the liquid up to the boil and add the sour cream. Turn the heat down low, add the meatballs, cover, and cook gently for 15 minutes. The sauce will thicken. Taste for seasoning, add the chopped dill, and serve with the cranberry sauce and boiled or mashed potatoes.

Lovely all through the fall and winter, this jelly is a fantastic color. I'm not usually in favor of garnishes that you can't eat, but the frosted cranberries, though beautiful, are rather mouth-puckering. Leave out the syllabub and just top with some whipped cream if you want to make something simpler.

PORT AND CRANBERRY JELLIES
with port syllabub and frosted berries

serves 8

for the jelly:

2 cups cranberry juice

1¾ cups ruby port

3 strips orange rind

juice of 1 orange

1 stick cinnamon

½ cup superfine sugar

6 tsp powdered gelatine

for the frosted berries:

1 egg white

fresh cranberries

superfine sugar

for the syllabub:

⅔ cup heavy cream

1 tbsp confectioners sugar

juice of ½ lemon combined with 2 tbsp ruby port

I To make the jelly, put all the ingredients except the gelatine in a saucepan and bring to just below the boil, stirring occasionally to help the sugar dissolve. Turn the heat down and simmer on a very low heat for about 10 minutes. Meanwhile, put about 4 tbsp cold water into a small bowl and sprinkle the gelatine over the top. Leave it for a minute or so to turn jelly-like.

3 Pour about 25ml of the cranberry and port mixture into a small pan. It must be no more than warm. Add the gelatine and stir to help it dissolve. Once the the gelatine has melted, add it to the rest of the cranberry and port mixture.

4 Divide the liquid between 8 glasses, each with a capacity of around ½ cup, filling about four fifths of each glass so that you have room for the syllabub. Leave to cool.

5 Refrigerate the jellies to allow them to set. You should leave 6 hours for this, just to be on the safe side.

6 To frost the berries, beat the egg white a little with a fork, then drop the whole berries into it a few at a time. Shake off the excess egg white and roll the berries in sifted superfine sugar. Set aside to dry.

7 Syllabub is best made at the last minute, but it's very quick to do. Simply whisk the cream with the sugar, adding the liquids gradually. Don't overbeat the mixture—it should fall in luxurious folds. Spoon a little syllabub on each jelly and adorn with your frosted berries.

This is the finale to the Danish Christmas meal, served on Christmas Eve. In the past, there was just one almond hidden in the whole pot of rice pudding, and it would bring luck to the finder. Nowadays they are more liberal with the almonds. The Danes serve this dish with a berry compote, usually made with dried or tinned sour cherries, but I like it with the tartness of cranberries. This is too good just to serve at Christmas, so make it any time from October, when the first cranberries appear.

DANISH CHRISTMAS RICE PUDDING
with berry compote

serves 6–8

for the cranberries:

just over 2 cups red wine

1 cup superfine sugar

½ stick cinnamon

1lb 2oz (500g) cranberries

for the rice pudding:

10½oz (300g) pudding rice

just over 6 cups whole milk

⅛ cup superfine sugar

3 tsp vanilla extract

3oz (75g) slivered almonds

2 cups heavy cream, loosely whipped

1 To make the wine-poached cranberries, put the red wine in a saucepan with the sugar and cinnamon. Heat slowly, stirring a little to help the sugar dissolve. Put the cranberries into the wine, turn the heat up until the liquid is simmering, and poach slowly until the berries are tender (about 20 minutes). Remove the poached berries to a dish and reduce the wine by boiling until you have about 1 cup left. Let this cool slightly, then pour it over the cranberries. Remove the cinnamon stick.

2 While the berries are cooking, make the rice pudding. Put the rice, milk, and sugar in a heavy-bottomed saucepan and gently bring up to the boil. Turn the heat down low and leave the rice to cook, stirring it frequently, for about 15 minutes, or until the rice is tender and the milk has been absorbed. If the milk is absorbed too quickly —perhaps because your heat is too high—add a little more.

3 Stir in the vanilla extract and almonds. Let the rice cool, then fold in the whipped cream. Serve cold or at room temperature with the warm berry compote.

This recipe is from a grand old Swedish hotel, Hennickehammar's, in Filipstad. Even though the cake isn't at all breadlike, they toast it, which works better after you've kept it for a day as it isn't so crumbly. They serve it with lingonberries instead of cranberries, but the end result isn't that different. When they're in season, replace half the dried cranberries with fresh ones—they're lovely and tart.

HENNICKEHAMMAR'S TOASTED GINGER CAKE
with wine-poached cranberries

serves 8

butter for greasing the pan

4½oz (125g) dried cranberries

juice of 1 lemon

3 cups all-purpose flour

1 cup light brown sugar

1 tsp ground ginger

½ tsp ground cinnamon

½ tsp ground nutmeg

1½ tsp baking powder

¼ cup (½ stick) butter, melted

1 cup milk

1 medium egg, beaten

confectioners sugar, to serve

for the cranberries:

just over 2 cups red wine

1 cup superfine sugar

½ stick cinnamon

1lb 2oz (500g) cranberries

I Preheat the oven to 350°F (180°C). Butter a 2lb 4oz bread pan and line the bottom with greaseproof paper. Put the dried cranberries in a small saucepan and add the lemon juice. Bring to the boil, turn the heat down, and let the cranberries sit in the juice until they have plumped up.

2 Mix all the dry ingredients together in a large bowl and make a well in the center. Combine the liquid ingredients and pour them into the well along with the cranberries and their juice and stir, gradually bringing the dry ingredients on the outside into the well. Pour the batter into the buttered bread pan and bake for 50 minutes, or until the cake is cooked in the center. You can test by inserting a skewer—if should come out clean. Turn out onto a wire rack to cool.

3 Put the red wine in a saucepan with the sugar and cinnamon. Heat slowly, stirring a little to help the sugar to dissolve. Put the cranberries into the wine, turn the heat up until the liquid is simmering, and poach slowly until the berries are tender (about 20 minutes). Remove the poached berries to a dish and reduce the wine by boiling until you have about 1cup left. Let this cool, remove the cinnamon stick, then pour it over the cranberries.

4 Cut the cake into slices, then toast them on each side. Serve slices sifted with a little confectioners sugar, with the cranberries and their syrup and some vanilla ice cream, crème fraîche, or whipped cream on the side.

This is not completely true to the Scottish dish, as I like to use some Greek yogurt instead of all cream, which I find a bit cloying, and I caramelize the oats.

BRAMBLE CRANACHAN

serves 4

2 tbsp butter

½ cup rolled oats

⅛ cup superfine sugar

⅔ cup heavy cream

½ cup Greek yogurt

2 tbsp honey, whiskey and superfine sugar

10oz (280g) blackberries

1 Melt the butter in small pan, add the oats, and cook for a minute, then add the sugar. Stir until the oats become caramelized, then tip them onto a piece of greaseproof paper and leave to cool.

2 Whip the cream lightly. Fold in the yogurt and add the honey, whiskey, sugar, and most of the oats (keep some back to sprinkle on top of each serving). Stir in the blackberries, crushing some so that they slightly break and stain the cream, but leave others whole.

3 Divide the mixture between 6 glasses. Drizzle with a little *crème de mûre*, if you want, and sprinkle with the rest of the oats.

"Late August, given heavy rain and sun
For a full week, the blackberries would ripen.
At first, just one, a glossy purple clot
Among others, red, green, hard as a knot.
You ate that first one and its flesh was sweet
Like thickened wine: summer's blood was in it
Leaving stains upon the tongue and lust for
Picking."

BLACKBERRY PICKING **SEAMUS HEANEY**

Bread-and-butter pudding, if made with fresh bread and good ingredients, is a great traditional British dish. The apples and cranberries really cut through the sweetness. Cook this all fall and winter, though it's perfect on Christmas Day for those who prefer something lighter than the British standard of Christmas pudding.

CHRISTMAS BREAD-AND-BUTTER PUDDING

serves 4

1 cup milk

1 cup heavy cream

pinch salt

1 vanilla pod, split, or ½ tsp vanilla extract

3 whole eggs, plus 1 egg yolk

½ cup superfine sugar

4 baby brioches, cut into slices ¾ inch (2cm) thick

2½ tbsp butter

good pour whiskey

3 heaped tbsp mincemeat

2¼oz (65g) fresh cranberries

1 small tart eating apple, peeled, cored, and finely chopped

confectioners sugar for dusting

1 Bring the milk, cream, salt, and the vanilla pod up to the boil. Remove from the heat and leave to infuse for 30 minutes. (If you are using vanilla extract, add it now and proceed with the recipe—there's no need to infuse or reheat the cream.) Beat the eggs, extra yolk, and sugar together. Remove the vanilla pod and bring the mixture up to scalding again. Pour onto the beaten eggs, whisking all the time. Preheat the oven to 350°F (180°C).

2 Butter the brioche slices and layer them, buttered-side-up, in an ovenproof dish, sloshing on a little whiskey, spreading the mincemeat and sprinkling on the cranberries and apple as you go. Pour on the cream and egg mixture through a sieve. Leave this to sit for half an hour—the bread soaks up the custard and makes a lighter dessert.

3 Put the dish in a roasting tray and add enough boiled water to the tray so that is comes halfway up the sides of the dish. Bake for 40–45 minutes, or until puffy and set on the top and light golden in color. Leave to cool slightly, dust with confectioners sugar, and serve with crème fraîche or cream mixed with Greek yogurt.

*"The moon, though slight, was moon enough to show
On every tree a bucket with a lid,
And on black ground a bear-skin rug of snow."*
EVENING IN A SUGAR ORCHARD ROBERT FROST

SUGAR SNOW
maple syrup

"How will I know which are the sugar houses?" I ask my friend Ed, a native Vermonter. 'Oh you'll know!" he laughed. "They're the ones that look like they're on fire." And indeed, all over the Vermont countryside were wooden cabins, some little more than shacks, with huge clouds of steam billowing from their roofs. I was in Vermont for the sugaring season, when sugar makers tap the maple tree sap and make their maple syrup. Driving in from Boston the night before, I'd caught my first sight of the galvanized collecting buckets hanging from the maple trees, lit by the moon reflecting off the surface of the snow. The practice looked even more earthy, pure, and old-fashioned than I had imagined, and I'd been waiting 30 years to see it. On fall afternoons when I was growing up in Northern Ireland, my teacher had read us Laura Ingalls Wilder's *Little House in the Big Woods* books about the life of a family of settlers in the late 19th century in Wisconsin. I had shared Anna and Laura's excitement as a "sugar snow" developed; the kind of snow that indicates the right conditions for tapping the sap. Later, their grandparents held a sugar-on-snow party when the syrup was boiled up and then poured onto clean snow, where it set in cobwebs of maple toffee. The idea of Americans still making sugar-on-snow like this seemed perhaps a little romantic, but on my trip I soon saw notices for community sugar-on-snow parties, when there would be warm cider, baked ham and potatoes, maple-baked beans, doughnuts, sugar-on-snow, and dill pickles. (Dill pickles are the archetypal accompaniment to sugar-on-snow, cleansing your palate before you take the next mouthful of toffeed maple.)

The russet color of maple syrup makes you think of it as the quintessential fall ingredient, but it's actually made in February and March. Native Americans, who were the first to make it, used to watch for the "sugar moon", the first sign that it was time to tap the trees. They boiled the sap right down, further than syrup, until it turned to granular sugar that was easier to store than liquid syrup, and for a long time it was the only form of sweetener available. There weren't many beekeepers to provide honey, and although molasses from the West Indies' sugar plantations became plentiful, it was pretty much boycotted by New Englanders as the trade in molasses supported slavery in the most direct way. "Make your own sugar and send not to the Indies for it," advised the *Farmer's Almanac* in 1803. "Feast not on the toil, pain, and misery of the wretched."

Willis Wood, a handsome bear of a man and a sugar maker for almost 30 years, is wrapped in layers of sweaters and clasps a warm mug of coffee. As it's the height of the sugaring season, he's boiling sap almost 24 hours a day, starting early, finishing late, and practically sleeping in his snowbound cabin. He sniffs the air, trying to ascertain whether the sap will flow today. Maple sap will only flow when it both freezes at night and goes above freezing during the day, so you never know what will happen. About 200 gallons of sap come into his sugarhouse every hour, but as it takes 40 gallons to make 1 gallon of maple syrup, he needs it all.

Willis tells me that, although the process of making syrup has become more efficient, the basic transformation of sap into syrup by boiling it down hasn't changed. "The sap itself looks just like water and isn't even slightly syrupy. It's amazing that anyone discovered what could be done with it", he says. "Trees generally have no more than three taps—more than that puts the tree under stress—these days made by electric drills. Into these we put spouts, and the sap runs through them into buckets."

Small-time sugarers, and there are plenty of "mom-and-pop" operators who manage to make enough to sell syrup commercially, and all "backyard" sugarers, who do it just for fun, collect their sap in this way, using buckets, but for more commercial enterprises, plastic tubing has come in big time. Squirrels and moose can gnaw through this, so it isn't completely efficient, but it cuts down on labor since nobody has to go and collect all those buckets, the vacuum system pumps out six times more sap than conventional taps, and the tubing carries the syrup directly to the sugarhouse. Once here, the work of making the syrup begins in earnest. Willis boils the sap in a large metal trough over a huge wood-fueled fire. He stokes the fire every 7 minutes and stirs the syrup, waiting for it to get to that optimum point when enough water has been boiled away and the syrup is ready to be "drawn off". Judging this is initially done by eye. Willis scoops the syrup up on a wide paddle and lets it drip, waiting to see if it is thick enough to "apron" or spread out in a wide, amber sheet. At this point the process is usually completed in a finishing pan where the sugarer can keep a closer eye on the temperature, and then the syrup is filtered and bottled while still warm. It's a labor of love and produces that rare thing, nowadays: a totally unadulterated food.

All this would just be romantic if it didn't also produce a fantastic ingredient. I didn't just fall in love with the idea of maple syrup early in life, I fell in love with its flavor, too, starting by pouring dark pools of it onto pancakes, then onto sautéed apples to go with ice cream and into pans of fudge. Used in nut-based cakes, for both the batter and the frosting, maple syrup enhances the flavor of pecans, walnuts, and hazelnuts and seems to make cakes that are particularly good for eating with a mug of coffee.

I now also use maple syrup in savory dishes, for example for making glazes, perhaps along with whiskey, mustard, or chili, to brush on roast pork, chicken, or sausages. In fact, it goes really well with all the ingredients we associate with fall and winter: pork, apples and pears, nuts and pumpkin (try drizzling a little maple syrup on wedges of pumpkin for roasting).

Maple syrup varies in flavor, the palest having the lightest taste, the darkest having the strongest, and its flavor is pretty much as you would expect if you look at the leaves of the tree: nutty, russetty, reminiscent of burned sugar and fudge. It makes the flavor of sugar seem dead and one-dimensional in comparison. I generally use the darkest syrup I can get my hands on—it has the most deeply nutty, mapley taste.

Before I left Vermont, I got to have my Laura Ingalls Wilder experience, attending a sugar-on-snow party with a hundred or so schoolkids. There were no dill pickles; but as we dived onto the maple toffee left by a barrel on wheels (a clever contraption designed by local sugar makers) we really didn't care.

I always forget how delicious spareribs are—every time I cook them I wish I bothered more often. These are great for around a campfire. And don't think that coleslaw is just a bland side dish. This one is a revelation. Use whiskey if you don't have any bourbon.

WILD TURKEY AND MAPLE-GLAZED SPARERIBS
with winter slaw

serves 4

2 racks pork spareribs, about 2lb 4oz (1kg) each

for the glaze:

⅔ cup bourbon (I like Wild Turkey)

5 garlic cloves, crushed

1 inch (2.5cm) square cube of peeled ginger, very finely chopped

7 tbsp dark maple syrup

2 tbsp Dijon mustard

2 tbsp Tabasco sauce

4 tsp Worcestershire sauce

salt and pepper

for the coleslaw:

14oz (400g) raw cabbage, mixture of red and green, thinly sliced

½ small red onion, very thinly sliced

1 tart green apple (such as Granny Smith's), cored and cut into matchstick-sized strips

⅓ cup sour cream

5 tbsp good-quality mayonnaise

3 tsp caraway seeds

1 Preheat the oven to 325°F (170°C) and mix all the ingredients for the glaze.

2 Line a big roasting tray with tin foil and paint the ribs on both sides with the glaze, keeping back about one third of the glaze to add during cooking.

3 Arrange the racks meaty-side-up in the tray, making sure they are not touching each other. Roast for half an hour, then reduce the temperature to 275°F (140°C) and cook the ribs for another 1½ hours, basting with more glaze from time to time. Add the last bit of glaze about 15 minutes before the end.

4 To make the coleslaw, mix all the ingredients, except the caraway seeds and seasoning, in a bowl. Toast the caraway seeds in a dry frying pan for about a minute, until the fragrance is released. Grind roughly in a small mortar and pestle and add to the coleslaw with some salt and pepper. Serve the ribs immediately with the coleslaw on the side.

"Maple sugaring will not be hurried. It is more than the work of one night or one week; its rhythms are measured in sunlight and shadow, in the tilt of the earth's axis and in the ancient memories of trees."
SUGARTIME WILL WEAVER

Pure New England. Maple syrup makes a great glaze, and you could try mixing it with mustard instead of chili. The cornbread recipe makes slightly more than you need, but it seems pointless trying to bake a small amount, given the size of cake and bread tins.

MAPLE-GLAZED POUSSINS
with cornbread and pancetta stuffing

serves 6

14oz (400g) cornbread
(see recipe below)

7oz (200g) pancetta

2 celery stalks, finely chopped

½ onion, finely chopped

1 small egg

leaves from 3 sprigs fresh thyme

salt and pepper

¼ cup (½ stick) butter

6 poussins (or small chickens,
about 1lb each, or small
cornish hens)

for the cornbread:

butter for greasing the tin

1½ cups all-purpose flour

½ cup cornmeal

1 tbsp baking powder

½ tsp salt

2 large eggs

1 cup milk

1 tbsp honey

½ cup butter, melted

for the glaze:

⅔ cup maple syrup

1 garlic clove, crushed

hot sauce (such as Tabasco),
to taste

1 Preheat the oven to 400°F (200°C). Butter a 9-inch (23-cm) cake tin. To make the cornbread, in a bowl mix together the flour, cornmeal, baking powder, and salt. In another bowl, combine the eggs with the milk, honey, and melted butter. Add the wet ingredients to the dry ones and mix, but do not overmix. Put the batter in the buttered cake tin and bake for 20 minutes. Leave in the tin for 10 minutes or so, then turn out and cool on a wire rack.

2 Preheat the oven to 350°F (180°C). To make the stuffing, crumble 14oz (400g) of the cornbread into a bowl. Cut the pancetta into meaty chunks and fry it in its own fat until colored on all sides. Add to the cornbread. In the same pan, sauté the celery and onion until they are soft but not colored. Mix with the cornbread and add the egg, thyme, and some salt and pepper. Fork the butter through as well. Wash the insides of the poussins well, dry with a paper towel, and season the insides with salt and pepper. Fill the poussins with the stuffing and tie with string.

3 To make the glaze, boil the maple syrup until it is reduced by one third. Mix with the garlic and hot sauce and brush or spoon over the birds. (You won't use all of it—keep some back for basting with.) Season well with salt and pepper.

4 Cook the birds in the oven for 50–55 minutes, or until the juices run clear when you poke a knife between the body of the bird and the thigh. Baste the poussins often with the cooking juices and the rest of the maple syrup. Serve immediately.

John McLure runs a terrific bakery and café in a big vaulted wooden building in Chester, Vermont. Cinnamon twists, maple-walnut bread, date bread—you just don't know what to go for. John makes these buns with brown sugar, but the addition of maple syrup gives them an extra Vermont flavor. Sweet yeasted breads can seem tricky (the amount of fat and sugar in the dough alters the way the yeast works, so you have to make sure the quantities are right for it to rise properly), but this recipe, which I have adapted from John's, works great. Perfect for a weekend breakfast.

BABA À LOUIS STICKY BUNS

makes 24

⅓ cup water, slightly warmer than body temperature

½ tsp dried yeast

¼ cup maple syrup

¼ cup (½ stick) butter, melted

1 large egg, beaten

½ tsp salt

4 cups all-purpose flour

for the filling:

2 tbsp melted butter

1 tbsp ground cinnamon

¼ cup dark brown sugar

¼ cup maple syrup

3oz (75g) shelled walnuts or pecans, roughly chopped

2oz (50g) raisins

1 Put the water, yeast, and 1 tbsp of the maple syrup into a bowl. Leave somewhere warm for 15 minutes so that it can froth.

2 Add the rest of the syrup, the melted butter, egg, and salt to the yeast liquid. Put the flour in a bowl and make a well in the center. Pour the yeast mixture into the well and gradually bring all the flour into the liquids, working the dough so that everything is mixed well together. Knead for 10 minutes, then put in a lightly buttered bowl, cover, and leave in a warm place to rise. You want the dough to triple in volume.

3 Preheat the oven to 325°F (170°C). Knock back the dough and roll it out on a lightly floured surface to make a rectangle 15 x 10 inches (38cm x 25cm). Brush the dough with the melted butter for the filling, then sprinkle with the cinnamon and brown sugar and drizzle on the maple syrup. Scatter the nuts and raisins on top, then roll up the dough like a rug, from the long side. Gently stretch the roll with your hands until it is about 24 inches (60cm) long. Cut the roll into 2-inch (5-cm) cylinders and place these in a buttered muffin tin. Bake in the preheated oven for 30 minutes.

4 When you take the buns out of the oven, tip the muffin tins upside down onto a wire cooling rack over a roasting tray so that the excess melted sugar can be rescued. Simply scoop it up and spread it on the buns as they cool.

I first read about sugar-on-snow, a kind of toffee, in Laura Ingalls Wilder's book, *Little House in the Big Woods*. Driving around New England in the maple-tapping season, you still see signs for sugar-on-snow parties where you can eat it with the traditional accompaniments of dill pickles—to cut the sweetness—apple cider and doughnuts.

SUGAR-ON-SNOW

serves about 15

2½ cups maple syrup

⅓ cup (5⅓ tbsp) butter

snow

I Heat the maple syrup and butter together over a medium heat. Turn the temperature down if it threatens to boil over. When a sugar thermometer reaches 235°F (113°C) cool slightly, and test by spooning 1 tbsp of syrup on to compacted snow. If the syrup sits on top of the snow and sets into weblike toffee, it is ready. If it doesn't, set it back on the heat to reach the required temperature.

"freezing winter night
        trees everywhere blossom
        with stars"

KEVIN CHRISTIANSON

Baked apples can be rather unwieldy-looking—big and rather gauche—but use rosy-skinned little eating apples and you have a rather elegant dessert. Replace the walnuts with pecans if you want a more American feel.

LITTLE BAKED APPLES
with maple and walnut ice cream

serves 6

for the ice cream:

1 cup maple syrup

1 cup heavy cream

2 tbsp whole milk

4 large egg yolks

drop pure vanilla extract

1½oz (40g) shelled walnuts, toasted and chopped

for the apples:

6 small to medium eating apples

2½ cups hard cider

⅓ cup dark brown sugar

juice of ½ lemon

I Pour the maple syrup into a small saucepan and boil until reduced by one third. Heat the cream and milk to scalding point. (Don't boil or the cream will split.) Beat the egg yolks in a large bowl.

2 Add the maple syrup to the warm cream and gently heat while stirring. Pour the cream onto the egg yolks, whisking as you do so. Heat this very gently—do not boil or the yolks will scramble—stirring all the time until the mixture has thickened enough to coat the back of a spoon. Immediately pour the mixture through a sieve into a bowl set in cold water. Add the vanilla and let the mixture cool. Stir the walnuts into the ice-cream base. Churn in an ice cream maker or still-freeze in a shallow container, beating the mixture about 3 to 4 times during the freezing process to break up the ice crystals.

3 Preheat the oven to 350°F (180°C). Run a knife horizontally around the middle of each apple and put them in a baking tray. Mix together the cider and brown sugar and heat gently until the sugar has dissolved. Add the lemon juice and pour over the apples. Bake for about 45 minutes, or until tender. Serve with the ice cream.

Maple syrup has a wonderful affinity with coffee—it may be its nutty taste—so this is perfect with a big steaming brew made with dark-roasted beans. It will make you feel as if you are sitting in café somewhere in New England.

HARVEST MOON CAKE
with maple syrup and pecans

serves 10

½ cup (1 stick) butter, plus extra for greasing the pan

⅓ cup light brown sugar

⅓ cup maple syrup

1 large egg

2 cups all-purpose flour, sifted

2 tsp baking soda

1 tsp each baking powder, ground cinnamon, and freshly grated nutmeg

1 cup unsweetened apple sauce (either bought or made from cooking apples and puréed)

3½oz (100g) pecans, chopped

for the frosting:

1 cup confectioners sugar, sifted

¼ cup (½ stick) unsalted butter, at room temperature

3 tbsp heavy cream

4 tbsp dark maple syrup

to decorate:

2oz (50g) shelled pecans

3 tbsp dark brown sugar

¼ tsp ground cinnamon

1 Butter the inside of an 8-inch (20-cm) springform pan and line the bottom with greaseproof paper. Preheat the oven to 350°F (180°C).

2 With an electric mixer, beat together the butter and sugar until light and fluffy. Add the maple syrup and egg and beat until blended.

3 Combine the dry ingredients (except the nuts) in a bowl. With the mixer on a low speed, gradually add the dry ingredients one third at a time, alternating with the apple sauce. Stir in the pecans.

4 Pour the mixture into the cake pan and bake in the preheated oven for 35–40 minutes, or until a fine skewer inserted into the center of the cake comes out clean. Cool in the pan, then turn out onto a wire rack.

5 To make the frosting, beat together the confectioners sugar and butter with an electric beater until light and fluffy. While beating on a low speed, add the cream and maple syrup. Using a silicone spatula, spread the frosting over the top and sides of the cooled cake.

6 To decorate, grind the pecans with the dark brown sugar and the cinnamon in a food processor using the pulse button (you want the mixture to be partially ground, partially chunky). Make a template of a maple leaf—or any kind of leaf shape that you find easily—by drawing one on a sheet of greaseproof paper and then cutting it out, so that you are left with the intact outline of the leaf in the middle of the paper. Set this on top of the cake and gently scatter the ground pecan mixture over it. Carefully remove the paper. You will be left with a sweet, nutty leaf shape.

INDEX